746.440952

WITHDRAWN

TEMARI

A Traditional Japanese Embroidery Technique

TEMARI

A TRADITIONAL JAPANESE EMBROIDERY TECHNIQUE

Margaret Ludlow

Guild of Master Craftsman Publications

First published 1998 by
Guild of Master Craftsman Publications Ltd,
166 High Street, Lewes,
East Sussex, BN7 1XU

ISBN 0 86108 080 8

Photographs by Dennis Bunn, except on pages
ii, 52, 53 and 135, by Michael Ludlow/
Line drawings by Simon Rodway

Designed by John Hawkins

Typeface 11/17 Sabon
Colour origination by Viscan Graphics P.L. (Singapore)
Printed and bound by Kyodo Printing (Singapore)
under the supervision of MRM Graphics, Winslow, Buckinghamshire, UK

Contents

THE DESIGNS

Acknowledgements

My grateful thanks to my sons Michael and Geoffrey for the computer.

To Michael for taking so much trouble and care with the initial photographs.

To Jim, my husband, for his patience, encouragement and help.

To my mother for living in Malaysia and having such cosmopolitan friends.

To my friend Sumiko Hattori for explaining the interesting history
and development of the temari ball.

To Coats Anchor threads for having faith in my project,
and supplying me with the Perlé threads.

Finally, my thanks to my 'crafty' granddaughter Victoria,
for inspiring me to get this book into print.

Introduction

ON a recent trip to Malaysia, I met a group of Japanese ladies who had come to my embroidery class to learn how to do unusual English patchwork. Without me speaking a word of Japanese, and they only a smattering of English, we were able to exchange embroidery techniques and I learnt the craft of temari. It was a wonderful experience. This book will, I hope, inspire you to rush home and try this ancient craft.

Temari balls are made from a plastic bag filled with polyester wadding, cotton wool or tights, covered with sewing thread and then decorated with Perlé threads in various patterns.

In Japan, temari balls are given to celebrate important events such as births and birthdays, anniversaries and weddings. They are often finished with elegant tassels and special temari knots (with which to hang them), and placed in glass cases for permanent display. After the hours of careful stitching involved in creating one of these works of art, it is not difficult to understand why.

CHAPTER 1

Tools and materials

TEMARI requires no specialized tools, and no expensive materials or equipment. The only new materials needed are the various threads (the tights, pop socks, and plastic bags used can be 'recycled'), and the 'equipment', such as it is, can be found in most homes. A basic geometry set is required – traditional temari patterns are all geometric designs – but the only other tools used are scissors, needles and pins.

TOOLS

Paper
A strip of firm paper is used as a measure (marker tape) to mark out the divisions and guiding lines on which each pattern is based. It should be firm, but flexible, as it needs to be wrapped around the ball. A strip about ¼in (5mm) wide is a good size to work with.

Card and plastic
Card or plastic is used to make templates for laying the guiding threads and then checking that they have been laid to the correct angles. Plastic cut from an ice cream container, for example, could be used.

Large, glass-headed pins
Pins are used as markers to indicate the various points around which the threads should be laid, stitched or wound. It is best to use large, glass-headed pins, as they are clearly visible, and the different colours can be used to distinguish the top of the ball (for which I always use red) from the bottom (for which I use black). Ordinary pins would disappear into the ball.

The tools for creating temari balls are very basic.

Protractor

The angle at which the guiding threads are laid is vital to the success of the design, so a protractor is needed to make card templates which are used to check that all the guiding threads have been laid to the correct angles.

Tapestry needles

As the threads used for temari are quite thick, the larger holes of tapestry needles are required. Tapestry needles are also blunter than dressmaking needles, so you are less likely to prick yourself!

Scissors

Be sure that your scissors are sharp.

MATERIALS

MAKING THE RATTLES

Rice, dried pulses, silver dragees, small bells or small pebbles

Any of these materials can be sealed inside a container to produce a rattling sound. Choose the filling according to the quality of sound you would like. Pebbles will produce the loudest rattle, and dragees give a crisp, clear sound, while lentils will give a softer, more muted sound. Small bells, available from craft shops, also work well.

Plastic bottle tops, lids, 35mm film canisters

Two lids, for example from plastic lemonade or milk bottles, can be filled with rice and taped together to create an effective rattle. Alternatively, you can fill a

The materials used to make a rattle.

Rice, dried peas, pebbles and dragees are sealed inside plastic lids to produce a rattling sound.

cut-down film canister with lentils or pebbles and seal with the canister lid. Any small container that can be covered with the temari filling without distorting the shape of the temari can be used.

MAKING THE BASE BALL

Plastic bags

Lightweight plastic bags are used to contain the stuffing of the balls, and provide a manageable surface on which to wrap the foundation thread.

Tights or pop socks

I use tights and pop socks, roughly cut up, as the filling for the balls. Polyester wadding and cotton wool can also be used, but I find the weight and feel of a ball stuffed with tights the most pleasing. Polystyrene balls look lovely when finished, but they lack the pleasing feel of a handmade ball.

The base ball of stockings bound with thread provides a surface on which to embroider.

***Cotton or polyester
sewing thread***

A foundation of sewing threads
wrapped around the filling
provides the surface on which to
stitch. Try to use threads with a
slightly matt finish to start with,
as shiny, silky threads are
more difficult to control.
Once you are proficient
at handling the
temari, this is not a
problem, but it is
best to avoid using
threads with a sheen for the
foundation as the decorative threads
tend to slip on these, which distorts the
design.

***Any colour can
be used for the
base thread.***

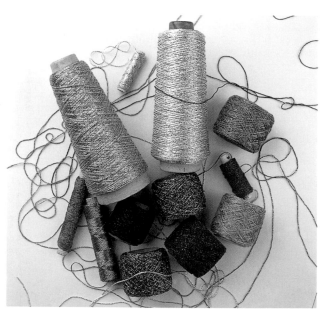

Metallic threads add sparkle and life to a design.

DIVIDING THE
BASE BALL

Metallic crochet threads
The guiding threads upon
which the different
patterns are built must be
clearly distinguishable
from the foundation
threads and from the
threads which make up
the design. Using metallic
gold or silver will add
twinkle and improve the
appearance of the design.

DECORATING THE BASE BALL

Perlé cotton

I have experimented with different threads for decorating temari, and find that Perlé threads give the best result: they are the easiest to work with, as the threads stay together when wound around the ball, and their sheen gives a lovely finish. Rayon, and slippery threads with a tight twist to them, need a lot more care to get them to lie as you want, and I would advise not to use them at first. However, for small temari, a thinner thread is required, and for these I use Madeira rayon threads.

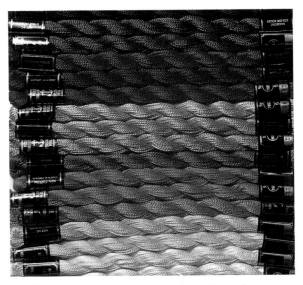

Perlé threads are easy to work with and come in a wonderful range of colours.

Refer to colour charts if you are unsure about your choice of colours.

Colour chart

If you are nervous about the choice and blend of colours, I have found paint colour charts (readily available from DIY shops) and colour wheels (available from art shops) very useful. They help you to see which colours work well together, and which colours contrast. As a rule of thumb, the base colour should complement the design, but rules are there to be broken!

CHAPTER 2
Making the ball

T HE base balls for temari are not difficult to make, and the special feel they have in the hand makes them well worth the effort. All that is needed is a little time and patience. Different sized balls are useful for making gifts such as key rings, earrings, rattles, pomanders and bell pulls.

If the ball becomes a little distorted, simply pummel it and roll it on the table, like moulding dough or Plasticine, and the shape will come right. If, however, it is totally out of shape, it is easier to start again. It is worth taking time to get the base right – I know, to my disappointment.

BASIC CONSTRUCTION

Put enough filler into a lightweight plastic bag to make a compact, orange-sized ball.

If a rattle is required, it should be 'buried' in the filling at this stage. (*See* Making the Rattles, page 4.)

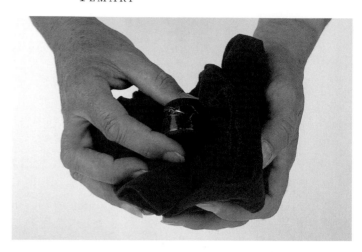

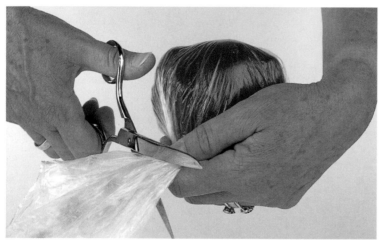

Wrap the plastic around the filling so that all the filling is enclosed and a ball shape is formed, then cut the surplus plastic away.

Flatten the cut edges of the plastic around the ball, as though wrapping a present. There is no need to stick the plastic in position as the foundation threads will hold it in place.

Wind the foundation sewing cotton around the plastic bag straight from the reel, like winding a ball of wool. You will need about two reels of cotton. Keep the threads taut at all times. It is very important to achieve the correct tension. If the tension is too tight, it will distort the ball. If it is too loose, and the ball is soft, the pattern threads will not lie neatly together and the surface of the finished ball will look bumpy.

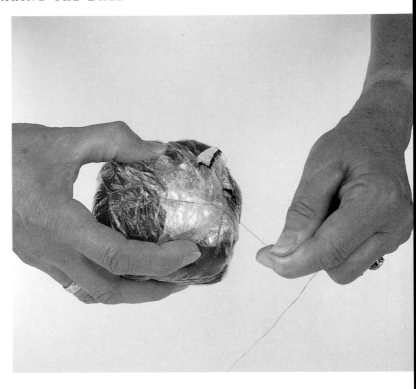

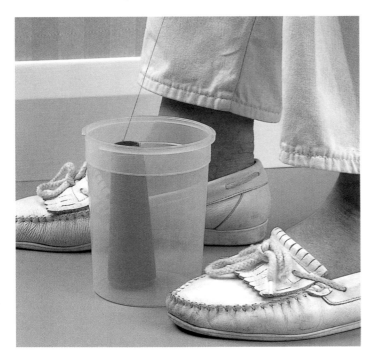

To keep the reel from bouncing away as you wind, place it in a container or jam jar. The tub needs to be heavy enough to withstand being knocked over by the bouncing reel.

As you work, pummel the ball in your hand or on a hard surface, to create an even sphere.

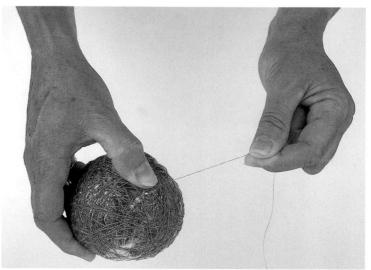

Turn the ball every now and then as you wind so that the whole surface is randomly covered and none of the plastic shows through. As you turn it, hold the loose end of the thread firmly in place with your thumb.

The tension of the threads compresses the filling so that, as you work, the ball will decrease a little in size.

When the plastic bag has been completely covered, cut the thread from the reel, leaving a good length to take long, random backstitches around the ball. I cut off a length that reaches from my chest to the floor. Turn the ball so that these stitches are made over the whole surface. Make about 15 to 20 stitches, then take the needle into the ball and out again about 1¼in (30mm) away. Trim the thread near the surface of the ball.

A comparison of base ball size according to amounts of filling used.

APPROXIMATE TEMARI SIZES

Pairs of tights	Diameter ball
Three	3½in (89mm)
Two	3in (75mm)
One	2¼in (51mm)
Half	1½in (45mm)
Quarter	1in (25mm)

CHAPTER 3

Dividing the ball

T RADITIONAL temari designs are built up from geometric patterns, which are repeated to create an overall design. In order to work a design successfully, guiding threads are laid on the base ball. These guiding threads mark out clear divisions and indicate where the pattern threads should be placed. The number of divisions used determines which designs are possible, as shown in the diagrams on pages 16 and 17. The designs in this book use between 4 and 16 divisions.

TOP, BOTTOM, CENTRE LINE AND OTHER DIVISIONS

The top, bottom and centre line around the ball are found using a paper marker tape. Handmade temari balls are never perfect spheres, so a new tape must be made for each one. A custom-made marking tape will enable you to measure parts accurately for a specific ball. Small differences in the dimensions around the circumference of a ball are enough to put the design out, and commercial measuring tapes do not accommodate these. Equal parts and accuracy are essential throughout the design.

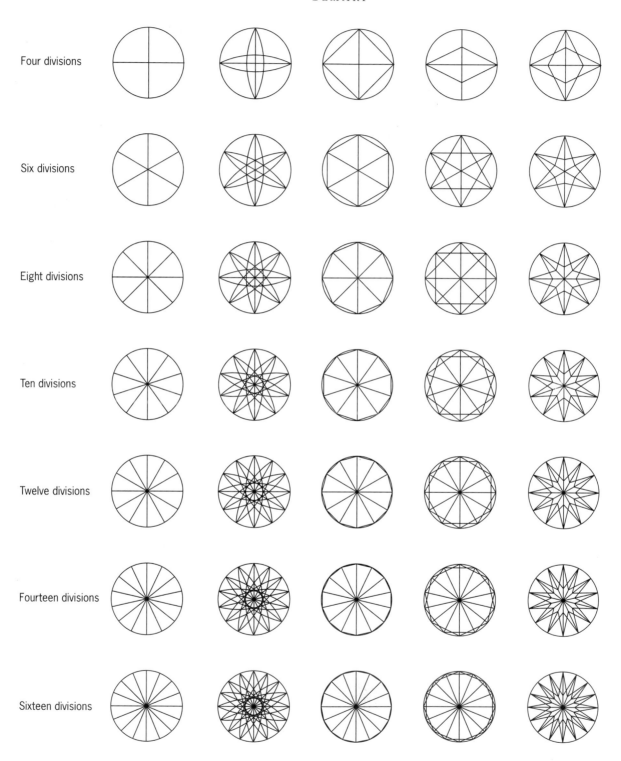

Design possibilities with even numbers of divisions.

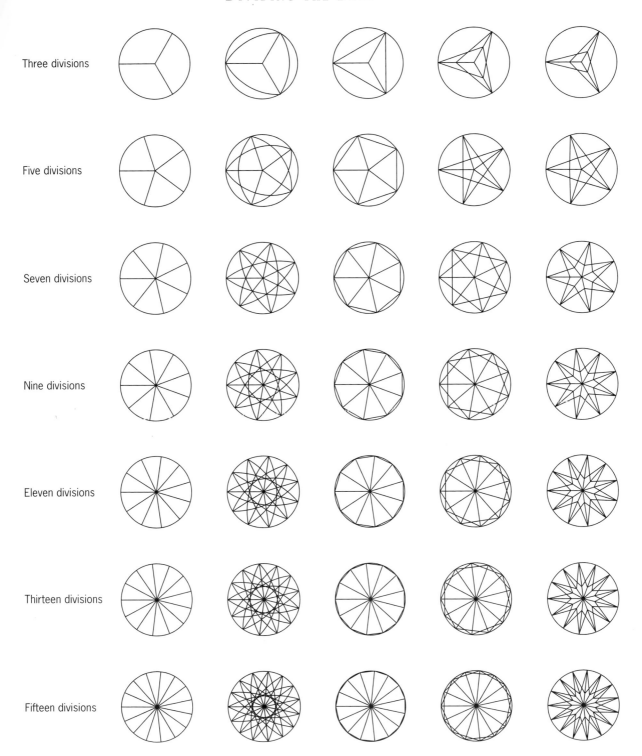

Three divisions

Five divisions

Seven divisions

Nine divisions

Eleven divisions

Thirteen divisions

Fifteen divisions

Design possibilities with odd numbers of divisions.

PAPER MARKER TAPE

Cut a strip of firm, but flexible paper, about ³⁄₈in (10mm) wide and long enough to wrap around the circumference of the ball, with a little overlap.

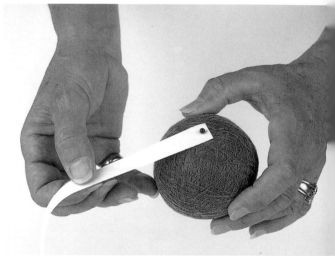

Attach one end of the tape to the temari ball with a glass-headed pin (red), leaving the pin head about ³⁄₈in (10mm) out of the ball. This will be the top of the ball. It is a good idea to always use the same colour pin for the top of the ball so that you know immediately which way up it should be held: if you put your work down for any reason, this can be a problem. I always use red for the top and black for the bottom of the ball.

Wrap the paper strip around the ball and back to the pin, keeping the strip taut. Bend the paper back at the point where it reaches the pin, and fold in a crease.

'Unwrap' the paper strip and bring the end over so that the crease is touching the pin. Fold in a second crease as shown. If you wrap the paper around the ball once more, you will see that this crease corresponds with the bottom of the ball.

Bring the paper over once more so that this second mark touches the pin, and fold in a crease. This crease indicates the halfway mark from the top to the bottom and is on the centre line of the ball.

Now bring the first mark on the tape over to the top pin and fold in a third crease. This marks the halfway point between the top and the bottom on the other side of the ball. Do not simply fold the paper in half and half again as the measurements will not be accurate for that specific ball, and the design will be put out.

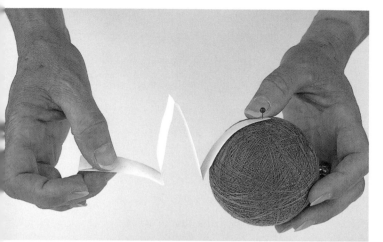

At this stage you will have a strip to measure halves. Continue folding and creasing each division in the same way until you have a measure for quarters, sixths or eighths, as required for each particular design.

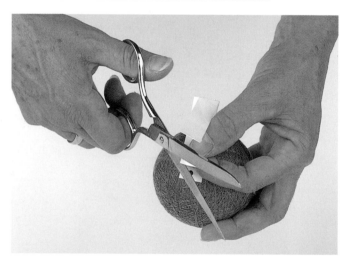

When all the divisions have been made, cut a small 'v' at each fold mark, taking care not to cut over the middle of the paper tape.

With the red pin still attached to the paper at the original top point, wrap the tape around the ball once more, and stick glass-headed pins into the ball at the 'v's, as directed in each of the specific pattern instructions.

FINDING THE DIVISIONS

When an even number of divisions is required, it is quite easy to gauge the divisions by eye, but this is more difficult for odd numbers: here the easiest method is to use an angle template. To find what angle you need to make your template, simply divide 360 (the number of degrees around the circumference of a circle) by the number of divisions you require. Thus for five divisions you would need an angle of 72°: 360 ÷ 5 = 72. Use a protractor to measure the angle accurately, and write in the size of the angle for future reference. It is easiest to work with a small template so that it can be held in place fairly easily. To help it sit flat on the spherical surface of the ball, run the template over the edge of a table or other hard edge once or twice to give it a slight curl.

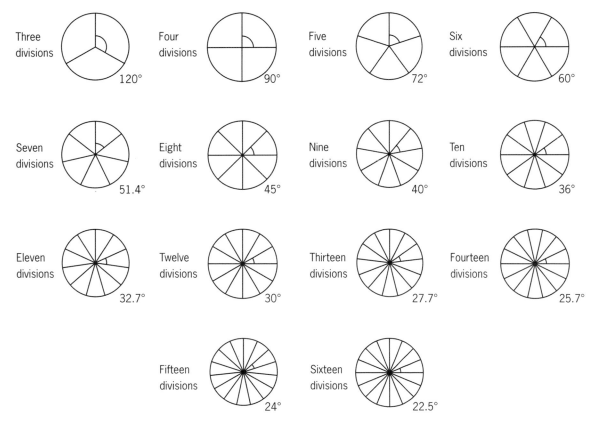

Three divisions 120°

Four divisions 90°

Five divisions 72°

Six divisions 60°

Seven divisions 51.4°

Eight divisions 45°

Nine divisions 40°

Ten divisions 36°

Eleven divisions 32.7°

Twelve divisions 30°

Thirteen divisions 27.7°

Fourteen divisions 25.7°

Fifteen divisions 24°

Sixteen divisions 22.5°

Table of angles required.

21

ESTIMATING THREAD LENGTH

To avoid wasting thread or, conversely, the annoyance of not cutting enough thread, I wind the thread roughly around the ball the number of times that is required, add a little extra, and cut that length. This thread can then be wound around a piece of card to stop it getting in the way while you work, and to stop it from getting tangled.

LAYING GUIDING THREADS

ODD NUMBER OF DIVISIONS

Thread a tapestry needle with a length of metallic crochet thread, and tie a double securing knot at the end of the thread. Metallic threads have a tendency to unravel, and a double knot will help to prevent this. Insert the needle into the ball about 1¼in (30mm) away from the top pin and bring it out at the top pin.

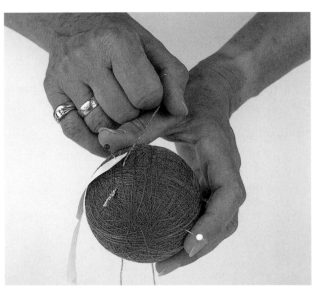 

Pull the thread so that the knot disappears into the ball. If it doesn't pull through easily, prod it with the end of the needle.

Wrap the thread around the ball so that it lies adjacent to the pins at the halfway mark and the bottom. Take a small stitch at the bottom pin so that you can take the thread back up to the top at the required angle. If you are using an angle template, place it at the bottom and take the thread around this, to the top pin.

 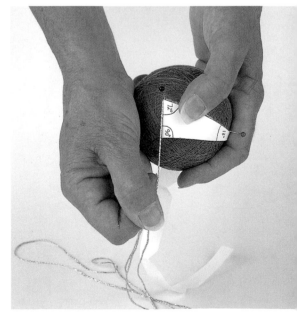

Pivot the thread around the top pin and take it back down to the bottom pin in the same way, using an angle template if required.

Repeat this procedure, pivoting the thread from the bottom to the top pin, then from the top to the bottom, until the required number of divisions have been made. Before you take the thread back up to the top for the final division, take a small stitch over all the guiding threads to anchor them at the bottom pin. Having laid the final guiding thread, secure all the threads where they meet at the top pin with a small stitch. Cast the thread off into the ball (*see* page 30).

EVEN NUMBER OF DIVISIONS

You can follow the same procedure for laying an even number of divisions as for an odd number, but it is quicker, and easier, to judge the angle by eye and mark in two divisions at a time by wrapping the thread right around the ball instead of pivoting at the bottom, then the top and so on.

The first step, always, is to bring the needle up at the top pin and wrap the thread around the ball, alongside the pins marking points around it, and back up to the top pin.

When you reach the top pin, take
a small stitch under the thread and
bring the needle out at the
appropriate angle to it, then wrap
the thread around the ball once
more. Continue this process until
you have marked on the required
number of divisions.

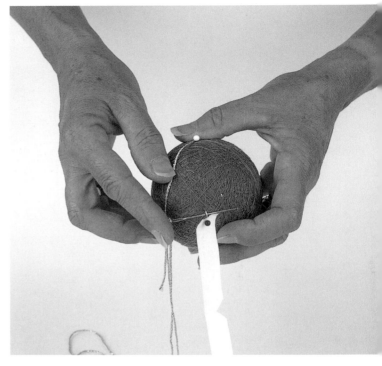

For numbers of
divisions that are
multiples of two,
this is simply a
matter of dividing
each section in half
and in half again as
many times as
required.

CHECKING ANGLES

With an angle template, check that all the angles are correct, and gently adjust the threads if necessary. If the angles are not correct, an uneven pattern will be produced.

MARKING A CENTRE LINE

If you need a centre line marked, insert the needle into the ball and bring it out at the halfway mark. You may need to take 2 or 3 invisible stitches into the ball to reach the centre line. When you reach the centre line, bring the needle up at one of the guiding threads.

Wrap the thread firmly around the ball and back to the same guiding thread, and then, looping under the guiding thread, cast off. To cast off, take the needle into the ball, as close to the last stitch as possible, and bring it out a little way from the design.

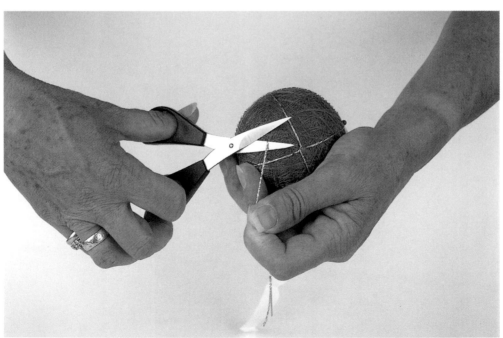

Cut the thread off near the surface of the ball.

CHAPTER 4

Decorating the ball

T HERE are three main techniques used to create all temari decorations. These may be used on their own or in combination. The techniques are:

- winding
- stitching
- weaving

For all three, it is important to keep the tension correct: if the threads are too tight they will distort the ball, and if they are too loose they will flap. The techniques for starting off a thread and casting off are always the same.

STARTING OFF A THREAD

Use the same method for starting off a decorative thread as for starting off a guiding thread. Thread a tapestry needle with a length of the appropriate colour, and tie a knot at the end. Take the needle into the ball, about 1¼in (30mm) away from where the first stitch will be made, bring the

Starting a thread: the needle is brought up at the point from which the first stitch will be made . . .

. . . and given a sharp pull so that the knot disappears into the ball.

needle up at that point (where the first stitch will be made), and then pull the thread so that it disappears into the ball. You are now ready to begin working the embroidered design.

CASTING OFF

Casting off is very simple. Take the needle into the ball as close as possible to the last stitch, bring it out again a little away from the design, and cut the thread off near the surface of the foundation threads.

To cast off, the thread is taken through the ball, a little away from the design . . .

. . . and cut off near the surface of the foundation threads.

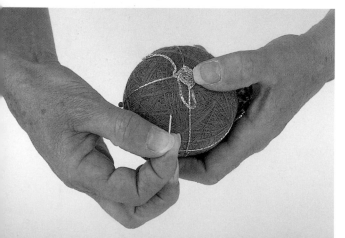

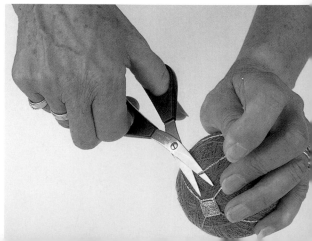

WINDING

This basic technique involves simply winding, or wrapping, the thread around the ball, under tension. Generally, a thread is wound around the ball a number of times on one side of a guiding thread, and a small stitch is then taken underneath these threads and the guiding thread at the top pin, in order to wind it the same number of times on the other side, in the opposite direction. A variation is to cross over from one side of a guiding thread to the other at a specific point, and then to cross back again at the corresponding point on the other side of the ball, as you wind.

Decorative threads can be crossed over guiding threads as they are wound around the ball.

The decorative thread is wound around one side of the guiding thread . . .

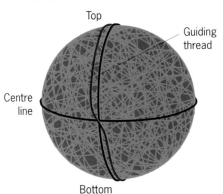

. . . then taken under the wound threads and guiding thread, to wind around the other side.

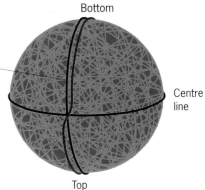

STITCHING

For traditional designs, three main methods of stitching are used, and these are shown below, but for free embroidery designs (*see* page 131) any stitch you choose can be used. For each stitching method, start the thread off in the usual way (*see* page 29). All the stitches are worked around the guiding threads. Always keep the thumb of your holding hand on the guiding thread and the decorative thread as you stitch to keep the thread under tension. This will keep the guiding thread from distorting, and the decorative thread from flapping.

As you stitch, hold your thumb on the guiding thread to stop it distorting, and on the decorative thread to keep the tension correct.

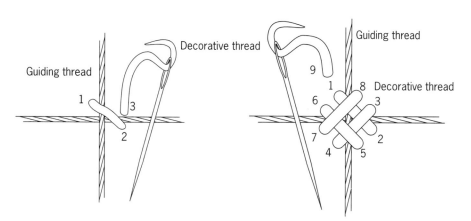

Placement and direction of stitches for stitching method 1.

METHOD 1

This method gives a square- or diamond-shaped pattern, and is worked around the intersection of two guiding lines.

Following the illustrations on page 32, bring the needle, threaded with the required colour, up at 1, down at 2, under the gold thread into the ball and up at 3, down at 4, under and up at 5, down at 6, under and up at 7 and down at 8. This is one complete stitch or 'round'. To build up the pattern continue in this way, bringing the needle up at 1 again at the start of each new round, and laying the new threads beside those already laid. This gets easier as the square gets larger, because the larger stitches are less fiddly to make.

Hand and needle positions for working stitching method 1.

METHOD 2

Method 2 gives an almond-shaped pattern. It is worked around one guiding line at a time. Rotate the ball anticlockwise as each stitch is finished, so that each new stitch is taken into the top of the ball. (Please note that 'top' here does not refer to the top as indicated by the red-headed pin, but to the half of the ball that is away from you while you work.)

Following the illustrations below, bring the needle up at 1 (to the left of the guiding thread), and down at 2 (to the left of the guiding thread). Take the

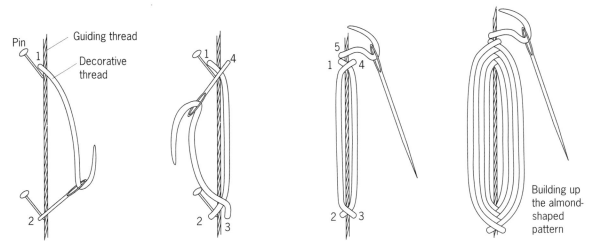

Placement and direction of stitches for stitching method 2.

needle under the gold thread into the ball and up at 3 (to the right of the guiding thread), then down at 4 (to the right of the guiding thread) to give one complete round. Build up a pattern by stitching successive rounds, with the threads of each lying alongside those of the previous round.

Use your thumb nail to keep the thread in place and under tension so that it does not flap. The thread must be held on the side of the guiding thread opposite that on which the needle is brought up and taken down. Remember to rotate the ball after each stitch so that each one is made at the 'top' of the ball.

Hand and needle positions for working stitching method 2.

The decorative thread is held on one side of the guiding thread and the needle taken down on the other.

After each stitch the ball is rotated, so that every stitch is made at the 'top' of the ball.

METHOD 3

A herringbone pattern is produced when you follow Method 3, with a plait formation at the top, and a 'v' shape at the bottom. This stitch is worked around the ball, over a number of guiding lines.

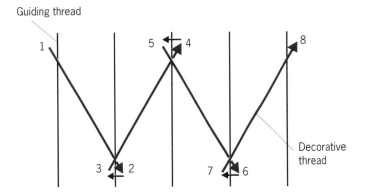

The plait formed at the top.

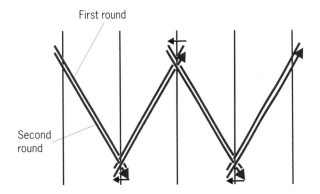

Placement and direction of stitches for stitching method 3.

The 'v' formed at the bottom.

Following the illustration above, bring the needle up at 1, down at 2, under the gold thread into the ball and up at 3, down at 4, under and up at 5, down at 6, under and up at 7 and so on, continuing in this manner over the area of the ball that is to be covered. A pattern is built up by bringing the needle up at 1 again and repeating the whole process, each time laying the new threads alongside those of the previous round and placing all the stitches below

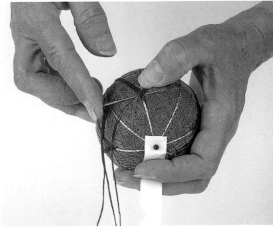

Hand and needle positions for the plait at the top.

Hand and needle positions for the 'v' at the bottom.

those previously laid at the top and bottom points of the pattern: this is what forms the plait at the top and the 'v' at the bottom. Unless otherwise instructed, all new threads should be laid over those previously laid.

WEAVING

Weaving is combined with the stitching and winding methods to give patterns formed by threads passing over and under one another. Where threads are being laid on an area of the ball that has already been covered, they can be laid on top of the original threads so that the new threads are seen, or the needle can be passed underneath the original threads so that the original threads

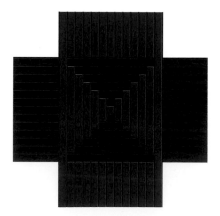

Different patterns can be created through weaving.

are shown. To produce interweaving, the new threads are laid alternately over and under the original threads.

To weave threads under previously laid threads, simply pass the needle under the required number of threads.

NEGATIVE SPACE

'Negative space' refers to areas of the temari that are not covered by the decorative stitches. These spaces can be left blank, their shapes being a design element in themselves, or they can be 'filled in' with a series of simple, straight stitches and patterns.

Making a series of stitches to fill a negative space.

Take the needle through the ball to move to the next negative space.

General stitching tips

A Whatever technique you are using, always place the thumb of your holding hand on the guiding threads over which you are working so that they don't become distorted.

B Turn the ball anticlockwise as you stitch so that you are always working on the half of the ball that is away from you.

C Thread will start to curl as you stitch and this will lead to knots. To prevent knots forming, let go of the needle and let it hang from the ball every now and then so that it can unravel.

D With some threads the strands tend to unravel as you work. If this happens, the threads will not lie flat on the ball and small buckles may appear, which will spoil the effect of the design. Check your threads regularly as you stitch, and gently work the natural twist back in if it has started to unravel.

E If you are going to use the gold or a coloured thread again later in the same area of a design, don't cast off: take the needle into the ball, as close to the last stitch as possible, and bring it out again a little way away from the design. Rest the needle in the ball, where it can stay until you are ready to use it again. To 're-start' it, just take the needle into the ball again, and bring it up at the required point. If you are going to use it again, but on another area of the ball, it is often easier to cast off, so that you don't have to work around it.

F As you stitch, keep checking that the shape of the design is coming out as you intend, and use the angle template regularly to check that the guiding threads haven't been distorted.

G Always keep the threads under tension, and place them carefully alongside the previously laid threads, guiding them with your fingers. Ensure that they lie flat, alongside one another: they should not overlap, nor should there be any gaps.

H It can be quite fiddly to work around pins in the ball. When you have completed the first stitch around a pin, remove it – the laid thread will now be your guide.

I If you run out of thread before you have finished with that colour, simply cast off, then start a new thread, bringing the needle up where the last stitch was made.

J It is useful to have a number of needles so that you can keep colours that are 'on hold' threaded and not have to keep unthreading and rethreading with each new colour that you use.

CHAPTER 5

Finishing touches

T ASSELS can be added to the base of temari balls for extra decoration. They can be made in a number of ways, with more complicated examples using beads and other 'formers' to give a solid, shaped head. Tassels themselves can be decorated with beads, stitching, braiding, and even mini tassels. All that is required here, however, is a simple thread tassel. To make one you will need:

- thread;
- a thin book or piece of firm card;
- scissors; and
- a needle.

To hang your temari ball, you can simply attach a length of thread or cord to the top of the ball with small, firm stitches. You can match the colours in the ball by twisting two or three strands together or use a single colour. For a more decorative, traditional hanging cord, try tying a temari knot.

HOME-MADE TASSEL

If you are using a book, find one that is about 7in (178mm) high and quite thin. If you are using card, cut a section 7in (178mm) high. Take a 10g (c. ⅓oz) ball of Perlé thread in a colour that relates to the temari ball, and wind the thread around the book or card about 50 times, finishing at the edge from which you began.

Cut a length of the same thread about 36in (914mm) long and double it, by folding in half, to give it extra strength. This will form the securing thread, which should be longer than the threads of the tassel. Pass it under the wound threads at the end opposite the starting end.

Secure with a tight reef knot. (For a reef knot, tie one knot by passing the left thread over the right, then a second knot, passing the right thread over the left, and then pull tight.)

When the knot is secure, pass the scissors through the wound threads at the end opposite the securing thread. Cut the wound threads evenly by pressing the scissors down on them.

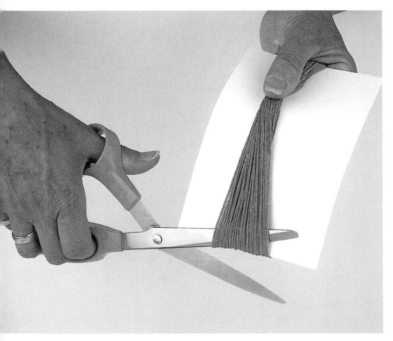

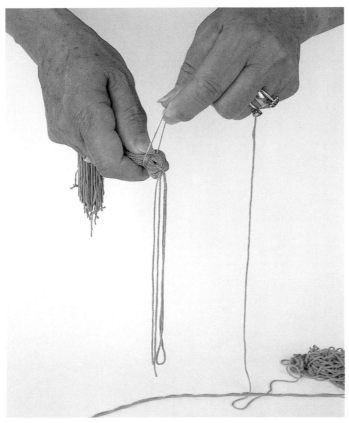

Cut another length of the same thread, 12in (305mm) long. Pull the wound threads taut, and wind this length of thread around them, about 1/2in (13mm) from the top. Secure with a reef knot, and trim the ends of this thread so that its edges meet the ends of the other tassel threads. This forms the first 'head'.

Holding the tassel by the original securing threads, turn the cut threads over the head so that they cover it neatly and evenly.

Cut another 12in (305mm) length of the same thread, wind it around the base of the covered head several times, secure it tightly with a reef knot, and trim the ends.

Turn the threads over once more to cover this second head, holding the tassel by the original securing threads, and stroke them into place so that they lie neatly around it. (It is worth taking a little time over this.)

Wind yet another 12in (305mm) length of thread around the wound threads below the second head, securing it tightly with a reef knot. Trim the ends neatly.

Take a piece of straight-sided paper and wrap it tightly around the wound threads. Slide the paper down the tassel until the bottom edge reaches the shortest thread.

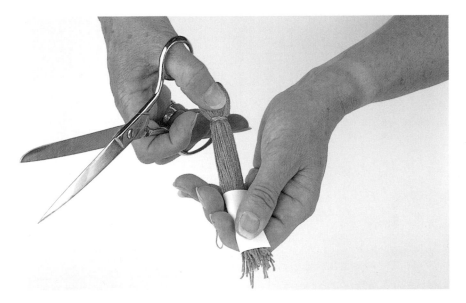

Trim the other threads with sharp scissors to match this, to give the tassel a neat and even edge.

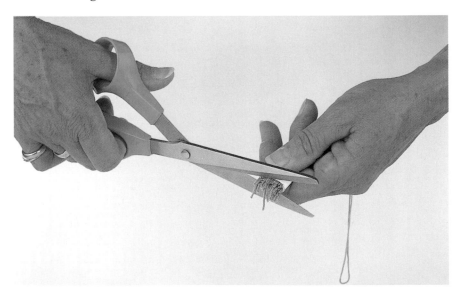

You can attach the tassel so that the head either touches the base of the ball or hangs below the ball. To have the head touching the ball, attach the tassel head directly to the ball with a few small, firm, securing stitches. To hang the head below the ball, attach the original securing threads of the tassel to the ball with firm stitches.

Temari knot

Take about 1yd (1m) of thread and lay it out on a flat surface.

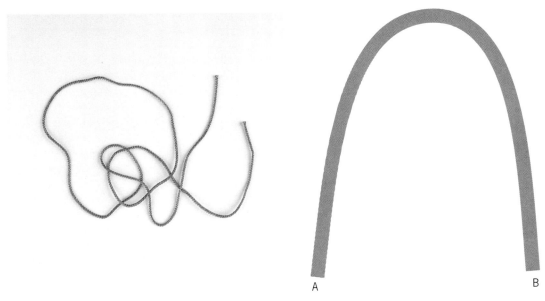

Take the end labelled B and pass it under the other side of the thread at 1, over at 2, and under at 3. Pull the thread gently to give the shape shown, but do not pull the knot tight yet.

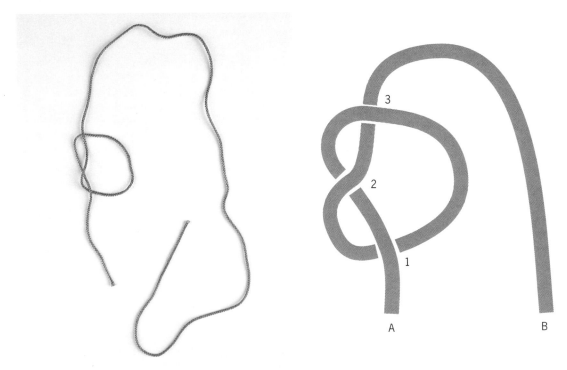

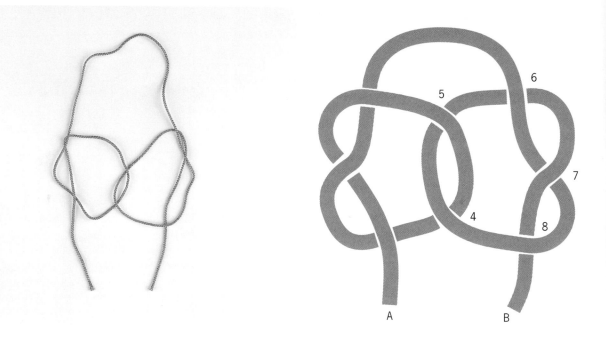

To form the second loop, pass the same end of the thread (B) over the first loop at 4, under at 5, under again at 6, over at 7, and under at 8. Pull the thread gently to give the shape shown, but do not pull tight.

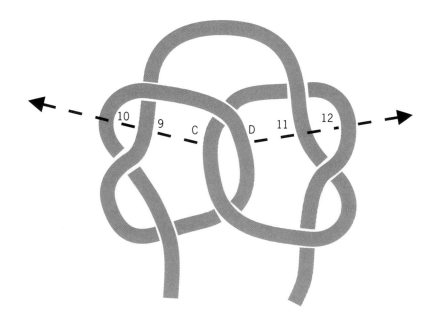

Now take the part of the first loop that is labelled C, and pass it under at 9 and over at 10.

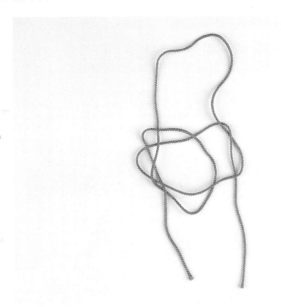

Next, take the part of the second loop labelled D, and pass this over at 11 and under at 12.

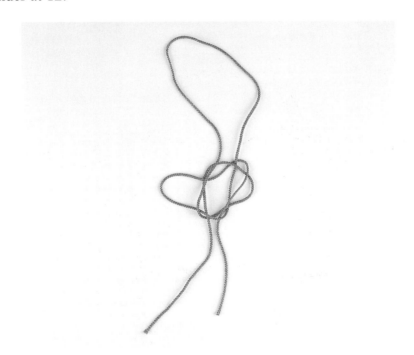

Gently draw these two sections out to pull the knot tight, making sure that it is even and flat. You should now have a knot with one long top loop and two shorter side loops.

Finished knot

Attach the long top loop to the temari with small, firm stitches.

THE DESIGNS

A s all the temari balls on which these designs have been stitched
are handmade, the size of the ball on which you stitch will vary
from them to some extent. Because of this, the number of rounds of
each stitch that I have used may not 'fit' your ball. This is easily
remedied: if your ball is smaller, simply reduce the number of rounds
to fill the equivalent space and conversely, if it is larger, increase the
number of rounds. I have listed the size of the ball that I used for each
particular design.

I have also listed the number of colours used. As I have mentioned,
I always use metallic threads, both for the guiding threads and to add
sparkle to the design, so I have not included metallic threads in this
colour count.

Each design has been given a difficulty rating as follows:

✳   easy
✳ ✳   moderately easy
✳ ✳ ✳   some experience required

CHAPTER 6

Stitching method 1, Stitching method 2, and Winding

DESIGN ONE

Difficulty rating: ✻   Colours: Three
Techniques: Stitching   Design size: Two pairs of tights
Divisions: Four   3in (75mm)

1 Divide the ball into 4 with metallic thread and mark the centre line.

2 With the first colour, bring the needle up very close to the point where thread 1 crosses the centre line, on the left of thread 1, as indicated by A on the illustration below. From this starting point, work 10 complete rounds using stitching method 1. Make sure that the crossing point, and the pattern formed, stay square, and that the threads lie side by side.

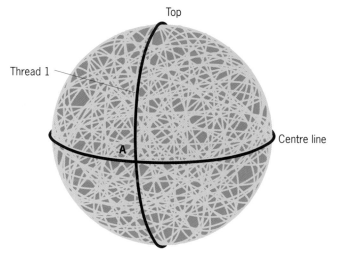

The starting point – 'A'.

3 Change back to metallic thread and complete 1 more round using stitching method 1.

4 Change to the second colour and work 5 more rounds.

5 Work another round in metallic thread.

6 Change to the third colour and work 5 complete rounds.

7 Again, outline this with 1 round in metallic thread.

8 Changing back to the first colour, work another 3 rounds.

9 Outline this with 1 round in metallic thread.

10 Work 2 more rounds in the second colour, and 1 more round in metallic thread. This should fill one-quarter of the ball's surface: work more or less rounds as required.

11 Once you have found the perfect number of rounds, turn the ball to work on the crossing point between thread 2 and the centre line and repeat the entire design.

12 Repeat the design at each crossing point around the ball. There are 6 patterns to be worked.

13 In the negative spaces that are left, mark the centre points, and make 1 long stitch in metallic thread, from one centre point to the next.

DESIGN TWO

Difficulty rating: ☀   Colours: Five
Techniques: Stitching and weaving   Design size: Two pairs of tights
Divisions: Four   3in (75mm)

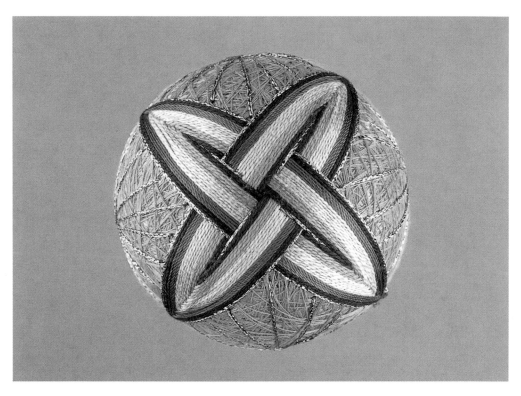

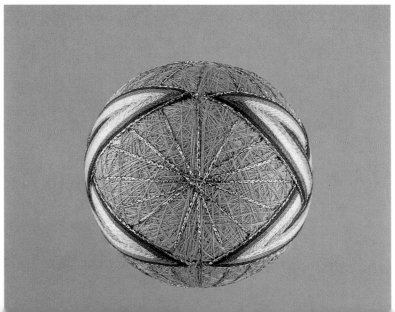

1 Divide the ball into 4 with metallic thread.

2 Make a marker tape to measure quarters, and place pins at these points on the guiding threads.

3 Using stitching method 2, thread the needle with the first colour and work 2 complete rounds, making the first stitch at the ¼ point on thread 1, and the second stitch at the ¾ point on thread 1 (*see* below).

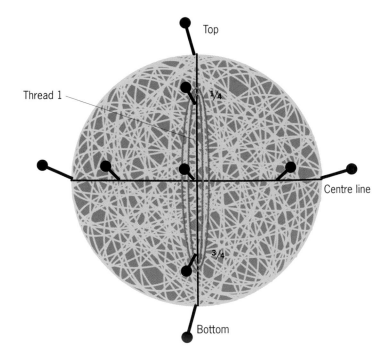

Top

Thread 1

¼

Centre line

¾

Bottom

The ¼ points on all the guiding threads are marked with pins.

4 Change to the second colour and work another 5 rounds.

5 Work 4 more rounds in the third colour.

6 Change to the fourth colour and work 5 more rounds, then work another 5 in the fifth colour and a final 2 in the first colour.

7 Work 1 complete round in the metallic thread.

8 Turn the ball 90° anticlockwise and repeat the process from step 3 to step 7, laying the new threads over the previously laid threads when working towards the guiding thread in the centre of the laid design, and weaving them under as you work away from it. (*See* below.)

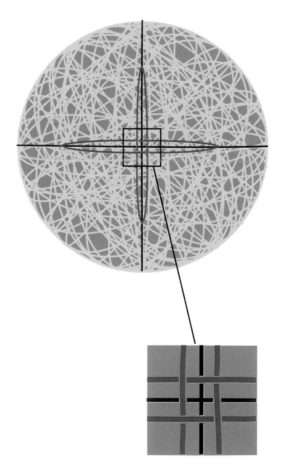

The pattern of weaving when the ball is first turned.

9 In the negative spaces that are left, mark the centre points, and work radiating stitches from these to the threads of the main design.

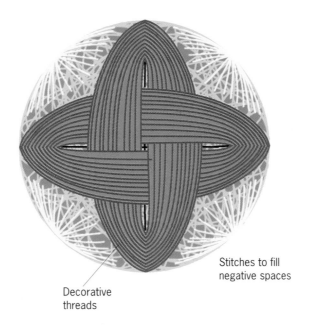

Decorative
threads

Stitches to fill
negative spaces

Large stitches, radiating from the central points, decorate the negative spaces.

DESIGN THREE

Difficulty rating: ☀

Techniques: Stitching

Divisions: Eight

Colours: Four

Design size: Two pairs of tights
3in (75mm)

1   Divide the ball into 8 with metallic thread.

2   Make a marker tape to measure quarters and place pins at these points on the guiding threads.

3   Using stitching method 2, thread the needle with the first colour and work 4 complete rounds. Make the first stitch between the ¼ and ¾ points to the left of one of the guiding threads (*see* below).

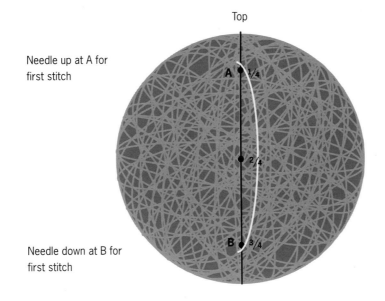

The design is worked from the ¼ and ¾ points on each guiding thread.

4   Change to the second colour and work 1 complete round in stitching method 2.

5   Change to the third colour and work 3 complete rounds.

6 Change back to the second colour and work 1 round.

7 Work 2 rounds in the fourth colour.

8 Work 1 final round in the second colour.

9 Repeat steps 3 to 8 in each of the 7 remaining divisions of the ball.

DESIGN FOUR

Difficulty rating: ✳ ✳
Techniques: Stitching and weaving
Divisions: Four

Colours: Three
Design size: Two pairs of tights
3in (75mm)

1 Divide the ball into 4 with metallic thread.

2 Make a marker tape to measure quarters and place pins at these points on the guiding threads.

3 With the first colour, work 6 complete rounds as follows. To start, bring the needle up on the left of thread 1, at the ¼ point (indicated by A on the illustration below), and take it down on the right of thread 1, at the ³⁄₄ point (B on the illustration below). Take the needle under the thread to the left side, and then back to the ¼ point on thread 1, but on the right side (C on the illustration below), to give 1 complete round. This will cover the metallic thread. Keep the needle threaded as you will soon return to the first colour.

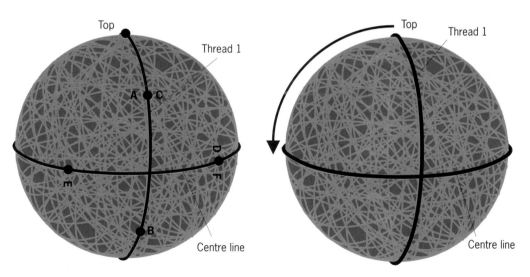

The design is worked from the ¼ and ³⁄₄ points on thread 1 (A and B), and from the equivalent points on the centre line (D and E).

Turn the ball 90° anticlockwise to work along the centre line.

4 Turn the ball 90° anticlockwise to work along the centre line (*see* above). With the second colour, threaded onto a second needle, repeat step 3, bringing the needle up midway between thread 1 and thread 2 (indicated by D on the first illustration), and down midway between thread 1 and thread 4 (E) to begin. Weave the new threads as follows: over 6 and under 6 to E, and then over 6 and under 6 again back to F.

5 Return to the first colour and to thread 1, turning the ball 90° clockwise, and repeat step 3.

6 Repeat step 4, following the same pattern of weaving.

7 Repeat step 5.

8 Repeat step 4 once more, weaving alternately over 6 and under 6 threads.

9 Change to the third colour, turn the ball to work around thread 1, and complete 6 more rounds. This pattern should now stretch from the top to the bottom of the ball.

10 Turn the ball to work around the centre line, and complete 6 rounds in the third colour. These threads should be laid over all the threads of the central patterns, but woven through the previously laid threads of the same colour as follows. For the first round, under 5 and over 1 up to the central patch, then over 1 and under 5 from the other side of the patch, and the same on the return. For the second round, under 4, over 2, over 2, under 4, and the same on the return. For the third round the weaving is under 3, over 3 following the same pattern; for the fourth, under 2, over 4; for the fifth under 1, over 5, and for the last round, over all 6. This band should now stretch from thread 2 to thread 4.

11 Turn the ball to work on thread 3 and repeat the whole design, from step 3 to step 10.

12 With the third colour, wind the thread 8 times around the ball, around threads 2 and 4. Use a marker tape to divide this band into 8. Place pins at all eight points around the band and make large stitches over it, from one pin to the next, crossing over from side to side. (*See* below.)

Top point of main design

Crosses over
central band

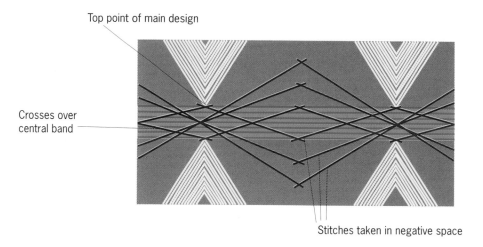

Stitches taken in negative space

Decoration on central band.

13 Turn the ball around to repeat this process from the other side so that large crosses are formed.

14 In each negative space, bring the needle, threaded with the first colour, up at a top point of either pattern, where it meets the central band. Take a long stitch down to the middle of the space, take a little back stitch to secure the thread, and then take the needle to the next 'top point'. Fill the 4 spaces on one side of the band in this way, then turn the ball to do the same on the other side.

15 Repeat step 14 with metallic thread, making the stitches a little closer to the central band. (*See* above.)

DESIGN FIVE

Difficulty rating: ☀   Colours: Three
Techniques: Stitching and winding   Design size: Two pairs of tights
Divisions: Four   3in (75mm)

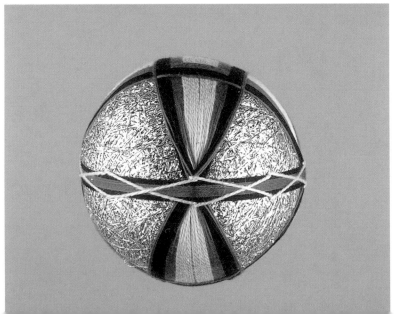

1 Divide the ball into 4 with metallic thread and mark the centre line.

2 Make a marker tape to measure halves, and place pins at these points on the guiding threads.

3 Thread the needle with the first colour, and bring it up on the left side of thread 1, at the top. Using the winding method, wind the thread around the ball, crossing over to the right side of thread 3 at the bottom, then back to the left side of thread 1 at the top (*see* below). Repeat this movement 8 times, each time finishing at the top. Make sure that the thread is always under tension, and that each thread laid on the ball sits flat against the next.

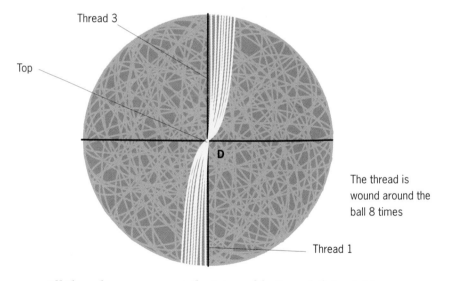

Thread 3

Top

D

The thread is wound around the ball 8 times

Thread 1

All threads cross over at the top and bottom: left to right from starting point A and right to left from starting point D.

4 Take a small stitch under these threads and the guiding thread and bring the needle up on the right side of thread 1 (marked D, above). Wind the thread another 8 times around the ball, crossing over to the left of thread 3 at the bottom, and back to the right of thread 1 at the top.

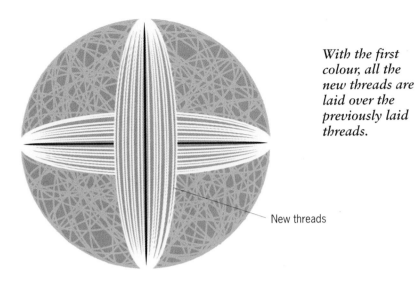

With the first colour, all the new threads are laid over the previously laid threads.

New threads

5 Turn the ball so that you can work on threads 2 and 4. Repeat steps 3 and 4, crossing over at the top and bottom as before, and laying all the new threads over the previously laid threads (*see* above).

6 Repeat steps 3 and 4 with the second colour, laying the new threads over those previously laid, then turn the ball and repeat step 5.

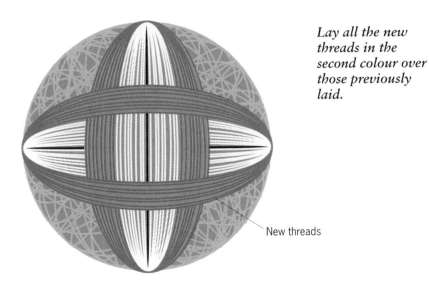

Lay all the new threads in the second colour over those previously laid.

New threads

7 Repeat steps 3 and 4 with the third colour, laying all the new threads over the previously laid threads.

8 Repeat step 5, laying all the new threads over the previously laid threads.

9 Outline the whole design with 2 more complete rounds in the first colour, laying all the threads over the previously laid threads.

10 Turn the ball so that you can wind thread around the centre line, over the 4 crossing points. Thread the needle with the second colour, bring it up on the left side of the centre line, then wind the thread around the ball 4 times, over the crossing points of the threads that have already been laid. Pass the needle under these threads and the centre line, and wrap the thread around the ball 4 more times, this time on the right side of the centre line.

11 Repeat step 10 with the third colour.

12 Returning to the first colour, bring the needle up in the centre of one of the crossing points, next to the central band. Cross over the band to take it down at the midpoint between this and the next crossing point. Take a little stitch into the foundation threads and bring the needle up again to cross back over the band, and take it down in the centre of the next crossing point. Take another small stitch, bring the needle up, cross over the band, and take the needle down at the next midpoint. Continue in this way until there are diamond shapes all around the band.

DESIGN SIX

This design is more easily done on a smaller temari.

Difficulty rating: ✳ ✳ ✳

Techniques: Winding and weaving

Divisions: Eight

Colours: Three

Design size: One pair of tights
2¼in (57mm)

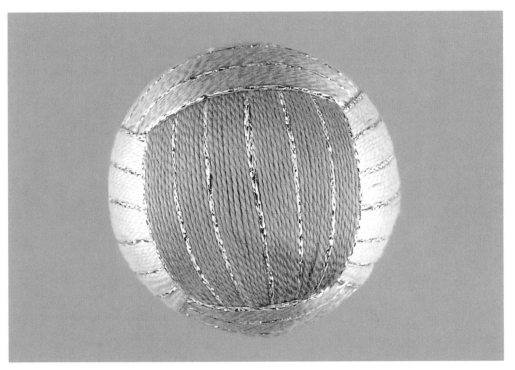

1   Divide the ball into 8 with metallic thread and mark the centre line.

2   Place pins at the top and bottom only.

3   With the first colour, bring the needle up on the left side of thread 1, as close to the top as possible. Wind the thread around the ball 8 times, crossing over at the bottom to the right side of thread 5, and back to the left side of thread 1 at the top. Keep the threads under tension and lying close together.

4   Change to metallic thread and wind around the ball once.

5   Turn and rotate the ball so that you can wind the first colour thread 8 times around the other side of thread 1 so that the threads cover the cross-over points.

6   Add 1 round in metallic thread.

7   Turn the ball back so that the top is facing and keep repeating steps 3 to 6 until the coloured threads reach guiding threads 2 and 8 on one side of the ball, and threads 4 and 6 on the other. (*See* right.)

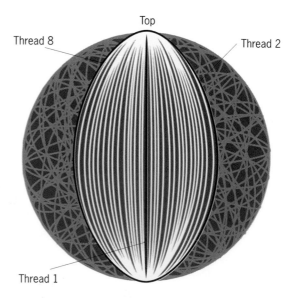

Placement of threads in first colour.

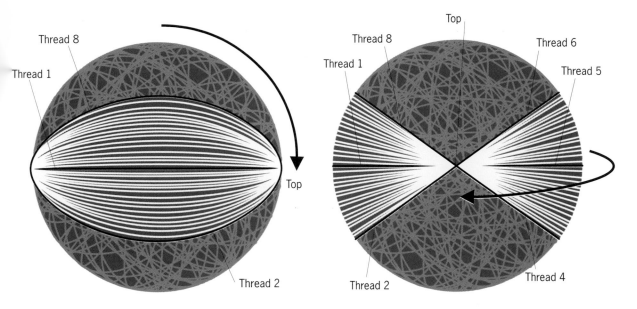

Turning the ball in order to lay the threads of the second colour.

8 Turn the ball 90° clockwise and 90° towards yourself (*see* above) and repeat steps 3 to 7 with the second colour so that the threads cross over from the left to the right of thread 3 and from the right to the left of thread 7, and the cross-over points of the first colour are covered (*see* below). Lay the same number of threads as you did for the first colour, and lay all the new threads over the previously laid threads.

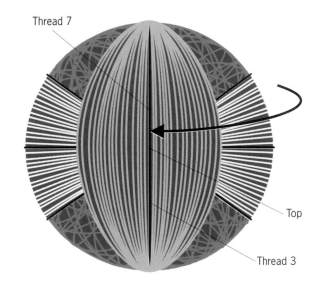

The threads of the second colour cover the crossing points of the first.

9 Turn the ball 90° towards yourself and repeat steps 3 to 7 with the third colour so that the cross-over points of the second colour are covered. These threads are woven under the first colour and over the second colour. As there is no fourth colour to cover the cross-over points, crossing over must be done under the previously laid first colour threads. (*See* below.)

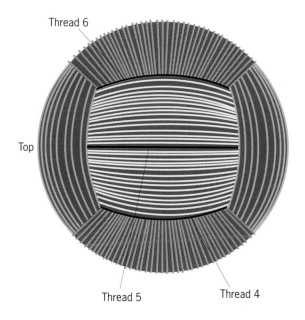

The threads of the third colour are laid under those of the first colour, and over those of the second.

DESIGN SEVEN

Difficulty rating: ✳ ✳
Techniques: Stitching and winding
Divisions: Four

Colours: Four
Design size: Two pairs of tights
3in (75mm)

1 Divide the ball into 4 with metallic thread and mark the centre line.

2 With the first colour, bring the needle up on the left of thread 1 where it crosses the centre line, and wind it around the ball, crossing over at the bottom to the right side of thread 3, and over again at the top, back to the left of thread 1 (*see* the illustrations below). Repeat this winding in a figure of eight movement, 8 times.

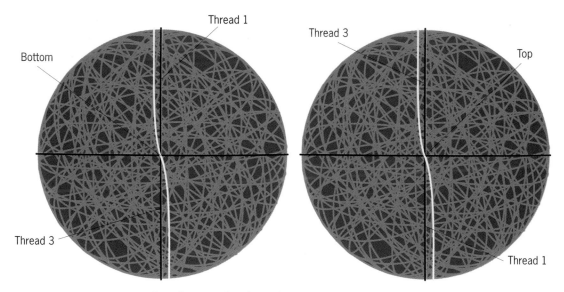

For this design, the threads are crossed over at the top and back again at the bottom, as they are wound around the ball.

3 Turn the ball 90° clockwise to work alongside the centre line (*see* top right). Change to the second colour and repeat step 2, bringing the needle up on the left of the centre line where it crosses thread 1, and crossing over from left to right and right to left where the centre line crosses threads 2 and 4. For this step and each step following, lay the new threads over those previously laid.

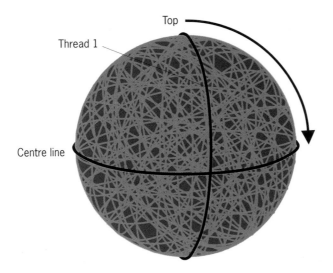

Top

Thread 1

Centre line

Turn the ball 90° clockwise to work alongside the centre line.

4 Turn the ball anticlockwise 90° and, with the first colour, wind the thread around the ball 5 times, to the left of the first 8 threads, then cross over at the top to wind another 5 rounds to the right of the original 8 threads.

5 Turn the ball 90° back and, with the second colour, repeat step 4.

6 Repeat steps 4 and 5, 5 more times.

7 Repeat steps 4 and 5 once more, using the third colour for both steps.

8 Wind the fourth colour around the ball, over the crossing points, 8 times.

9 Keeping the fourth colour, sew large cross stitches over the central band all around the ball, and then repeat the process, starting the thread on the other side, to form a series of diamonds.

DESIGN EIGHT

Difficulty rating: ✳ ✳ ✳
Techniques: Winding and stitching
Divisions: Ten

Colours: Five
Design size: Two pairs of tights
3in (75mm)

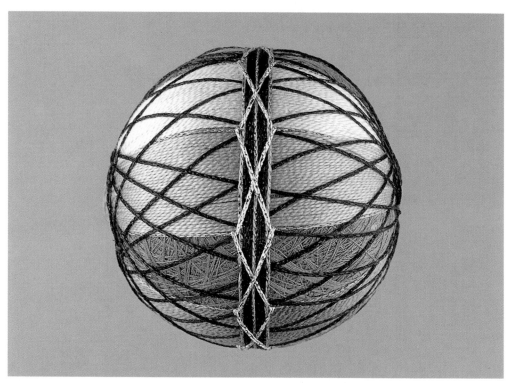

1 Divide the ball into 10 with metallic thread.

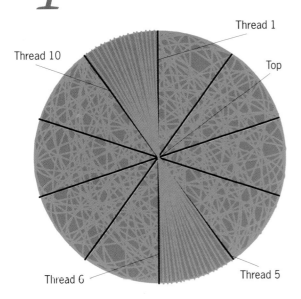

The decorative threads are crossed over the guiding thread, from one side to the other, at the top and bottom of the ball.

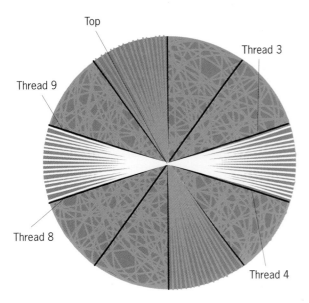

All the new threads are laid over the top of the previously laid threads.

2 With the first colour, bring the needle up on the left of thread 1, at the top. Wind it around the ball, crossing from the left of thread 1 to the right of thread 6 at the bottom and then back to the left of thread 1 at the top. Wind the thread around the ball enough times to fill the space between threads 1 and 10 on one side, and threads 6 and 5 on the other. (*See* left.)

3 Change to the second colour and repeat step 2, beginning on the left of thread 4, crossing over at the bottom to the right of thread 9, then crossing back to the left of thread 4 at the top. Fill the space between threads 4 and 3, and threads 9 and 8 with the second colour. Lay all the new threads over the previously laid threads. (*See* left.)

4 Change to the third colour and repeat step 2, but start on the left of thread 3 and cross over at the bottom to the right of thread 8. Wind enough threads to fill the space between threads 3 and 2, and

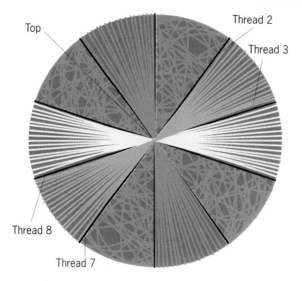

The third colour crosses from one side of the second colour to the other.

threads 8 and 7. Lay all the new threads over the previously laid threads. This band will cross over both the other bands at the top and bottom, crossing from one side of the second colour to the other. (*See the illustration left.*)

5 With the fourth, contrasting colour, bring the needle up about $^{3}/_{4}$in (20mm) from the top, and wind the thread, under tension, to the same distance from the bottom pin, a little further around the ball. Wind the thread back up to the top, the same distance away, a little further around again. Continue with this until the ball is encased in a basketweave, with an opening around the top and the bottom about 1$^{1}/_{2}$in (45mm) wide. Make sure that the thread is wound under tension the whole time. The tension of the decorative threads should hold them in position, but with handling the threads could easily be moved, so make a few anchoring stitches to secure the stitches for peace of mind!

6 Mark the centre line with metallic thread.

7 Change to the fifth colour and wind the thread 4 times around each side of the centre line, taking a stitch under the threads from one side to the other when the first half is done.

8 Return to the metallic thread and outline the central band with 1 thread on either side.

9 Still with the metallic thread, stitch across the central band from one guiding thread to the next, all around the ball. Turn the ball so that the bottom is facing and repeat the process from the other side to form diamonds.

CHAPTER 7

Stitching method 3

DESIGN NINE

Difficulty rating: ✳ ✳

Techniques: Stitching and weaving

Divisions: Five

Colours: Five

Design size: Two pairs of tights
3in (75mm)

1 Divide the ball into 5 with metallic thread and mark the centre line.

2 Make a marker tape to measure eighths and place pins at the $^1/_8$ and $^3/_8$ points on all the guiding threads. Work one half of the ball at a time.

3 With the first colour, work 5 rounds using stitching method 3. To start, bring the needle up at the $^1/_8$ point on the left of thread 1 (indicated by A on the illustration right), take it down on the right of the $^3/_8$ point on thread 2 (B), under the guiding thread and up on the left side (C), then down on the right of the $^1/_8$ point on thread 3 (D). Continue in this way around the ball until the needle returns to the $^1/_8$ point on thread 1, but on the right-hand side: you will need to stitch round the ball twice to return to thread 1 and to complete 1 round. As you stitch from $^1/_8$ points to $^3/_8$ points,

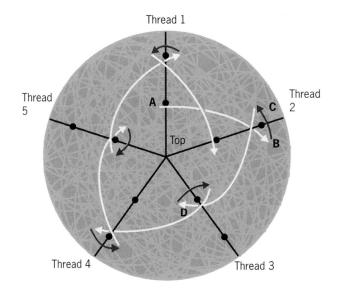

Placement and direction of stitches.

weave the threads over those previously laid, as you stitch from $^3/_8$ points to $^1/_8$ points, weave them under those previously laid, and as you stitch *at* the $^1/_8$ points, weave them over those previously laid. Place all the new threads below those previously laid to form a plait at the $^1/_8$ points and a 'v' at the $^3/_8$ points.

4 Change to the second colour and complete 3 more rounds in the same way.

5 Change to the third colour and complete 2 more rounds.

6 Turn the ball so that the bottom becomes the top and repeat the whole process from step 2 to step 5, using the same marker tape.

7 Wind a thread in a fourth, contrasting colour twice around one side of the centre line, then take a small stitch under these threads to come out on the other side of the centre line, and wind it twice around this side.

8 In a fifth colour, repeat step 7.

9 Repeat step 7 in the fourth colour again.

10 Return to the third colour to make large stitches in the negative spaces near the central band. Bring the needle up at a top point of one of the designs and down in the centre of the space, then make a small backstitch before taking it up to the next top point. Continue in this way around the ball, then work another round with slightly shallower stitches, taking the needle down closer to the central band (*see* below). Do this on both sides of the ball.

Large stitches in negative space

Cross stitch

Decoration on central band.

11 Staying with the third colour, make 5 cross stitches over the central band, between the top points of the two designs.

12 Weave the fourth colour 5 times around the top and bottom. As there is an odd number of guiding threads in this design, the weaving will follow the correct sequence without changing directions for each round.

DESIGN TEN

Difficulty rating: ✻ ✻
Techniques: Stitching and weaving
Divisions: Twelve

Colours: Four
Design size: Two pairs of tights
3in (75mm)

1 Divide the ball into 12 with metallic thread.

2 Make a marker tape to measure sixths. Place pins at the ¹⁄₆ points on threads 1, 3, 5, 7, 9 and 11, then place a second round of pins at the ²⁄₆ points on threads 2, 4, 6, 8, 10 and 12.

3 Using stitching method 3, work 1 complete round in metallic thread. To start, bring the needle up on the left of thread 1, at the ¹⁄₆ point. Take the needle over to the right of thread 2, at the ²⁄₆ point, rotating the ball clockwise. Take a stitch under thread 2 to come up on the left side, then take the needle down on the right of thread 3, at the ¹⁄₆ point. Continue in this way around the ball. (*See* below.)

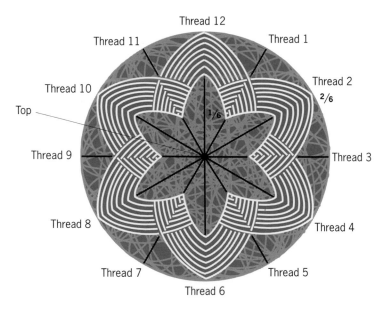

The basic pattern of stitches.

4 Work 4 more rounds in the first colour, keeping the threads very close together. This will form a plait at the top and a 'v' at the bottom.

5 Complete 1 more round in metallic thread.

6 Change to the second colour and work 4 rounds.

7 Add another round of metallic thread.

8 Complete 4 rounds in the third colour and add another round of metallic thread.

9 Work another 4 rounds in the fourth colour and add a final round of metallic thread.

10 Turn the ball so that the bottom is facing, and repeat the whole process, from step 2 to step 8. When the design is complete, the threads should meet up in the middle. If the ball is smaller than the sample shown, less rounds will be needed, and if it is bigger, more. A flower shape will be formed around the top and bottom, and diamonds will form around the centre line.

11 Weave metallic thread around the top and bottom of the ball about 5 times, changing direction for each round so that the weaving pattern is kept correct.

DESIGN ELEVEN

Difficulty rating: ✳ ✳ ✳
Techniques: Stitching and weaving
Divisions: Sixteen

Colours: Five
Design size: Two pairs of tights
3in (75mm)

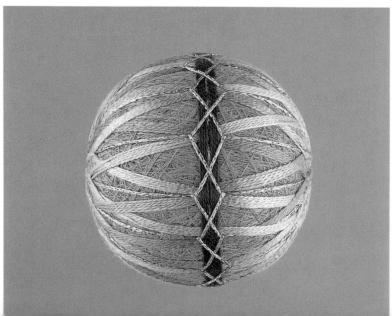

1   Divide the ball into 16 with metallic thread.

2   With the first colour thread, complete 5 rounds using stitching method 3. Start at the top of the ball and take a small stitch to come up on the left of thread 1 (indicated by A on the illustration below), then take the needle down to the bottom, on the right of thread 3. Take a small stitch under thread 3 to come up on the left side, and take the needle up to the right side of thread 5. Continue in this way, working on threads 7, 9, 11, 13, 15 and back to 1. (*See the pattern formed, below.*)

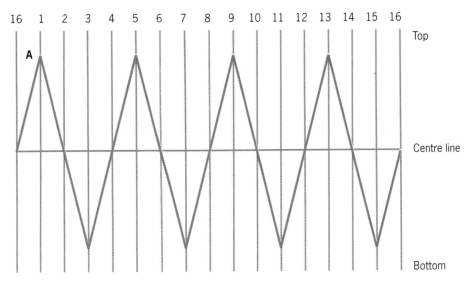

Placement of stitches for the first colour.

3   Change to the second colour and work 5 rounds in stitching method 3, starting on thread 2, weaving the new threads under those previously laid as you stitch from the top to the bottom, and over those previously laid as you return from the bottom to the top.

4   Change to the third colour and follow the same routine and weaving pattern, starting on the left of thread 3, at the top. Again, work 5 rounds.

5 With the fourth colour, work another 5 rounds, starting on the left of thread 4, following the same routine.

6 Lay a guiding thread to mark the centre line. Wind the fifth colour 4 times around one side of the centre line, take a small stitch under these threads, and then wind it 4 times around the other side.

7 With metallic thread, take stitches over the central band from one side to the other, making a stitch at each of the guiding threads. Turn the ball so the bottom is facing and repeat the process to form diamonds. (*See* below.)

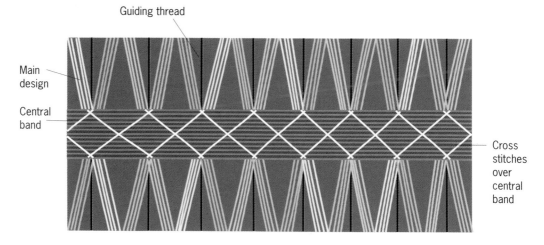

Decoration on central band.

DESIGN TWELVE

Difficulty rating: ✳ ✳ ✳	Colours: Six
Techniques: Stitching and weaving	Design size: Two pairs of tights
Divisions: Sixteen	3in (75mm)

1 Divide the ball into 16 with metallic thread.

2 Make a marker tape to measure quarters and place pins at the $^2/_4$ points on alternate threads, starting at thread 1.

3 Weave metallic thread over and under the guiding threads at the top and bottom of the ball. Complete 3 rounds, reversing directions with each round to keep the weave correct.

4 With the first colour thread, work 2 complete rounds using stitching method 3. To start, bring the needle up as close as possible to the top patch, on the left of thread 1, then take the needle over to the right of thread 3, at the $^2/_4$ point, under thread 3 and up on the left side, then over to the right of thread 5, at the top. Continue in this way around the ball and return to the top at thread 1 to complete 1 round. Lay all the new threads over those previously laid, and place each new stitch below those previously laid.

5 Repeat step 4, but start each round at thread 3 instead of thread 1. Lay all the new threads over those previously laid.

6 Change to the second colour and repeat steps 4 and 5, laying all the new threads over those previously laid.

7 Repeat steps 4 and 5 another 4 times, once each in the third, fourth, fifth and sixth colours.

8 Turn the ball so that the bottom is facing and use the marker tape to place pins at the $^1/_4$ points on alternate threads, starting on thread 2.

9 Repeat the whole process, from step 4 to step 7, but begin on thread 2 so that the long, petal shapes lie in between those of the first pattern, and take the stitches between the bottom and the $1/4$ point rather than the $2/4$ point so that the petal shapes of this design are shorter (*see* below).

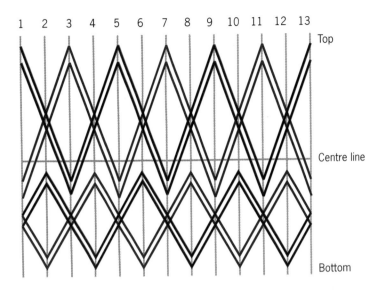

The top and bottom designs are stitched on alternate threads.

DESIGN THIRTEEN

Difficulty rating: ✻ ✻

Techniques: Stitching and weaving

Divisions: Ten

Colours: Three

Design size: Two pairs of tights
3in (75mm)

1 Divide the ball into 10 with metallic thread and mark the centre line.

2 Make a marker tape to measure ¹/₄in (5mm) and another to measure quarters, and place pins on all the guiding threads, at both the ¹/₄in (5mm) points and the ¹/₄ points.

3 With the first colour, lay 14 rounds using stitching method 3. To start, bring the needle up on the left of thread 1, at the ¹/₄in (5mm) point, and take it down on the right of thread 2, at the ¹/₄ point. Take a small stitch under thread 2 to come up on the left side, then take the needle over to the right of thread 3, at the ¹/₄in (5mm) point. Follow this routine, stitching on all threads back to thread 1 to complete 1 round. When all 14 rounds are complete, add 1 round in metallic thread. Lay all the new threads over the previously laid threads, and place each stitch below the previous stitches.

4 Change to the second colour and follow the same routine as for step 3, but bring the needle up at the ¹/₄in (5mm) point on thread 2 to start. Weave these new threads over the previously laid threads as you stitch from the ¹/₄in (5mm) point to the ¹/₄ point, and under the previously laid threads as you stitch back up to the ¹/₄in (5mm) point. (*See* below.)

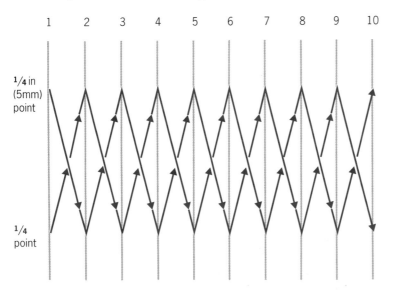

Placement and direction of stitches and weaving.

5 Turn the ball so that the bottom is facing and repeat steps 2 to 4.

6 Weave metallic thread 4 times around the guiding threads at the top and bottom, changing direction with each round to keep the weave correct.

7 With a third, contrasting colour, wind the thread twice around one side of the centre line, then take a stitch under the threads to come up on the other side of the centre line, and wind the thread twice around that side.

8 With the metallic thread, bring the needle up on the left of thread 1 at the central band, then cross over the band and take it down on the right side of thread 2. Take a stitch under the thread to come up on the left side, then cross back over the band to the right side of thread 3. Continue in this way around the entire ball, then turn the ball so that the top is facing, and repeat the process. (*See* below.)

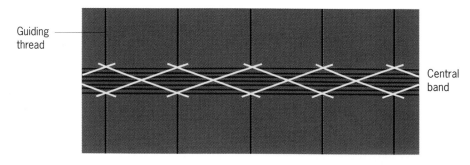

Decoration on central band.

DESIGN FOURTEEN

Difficulty rating: ✳ ✳ ✳
Techniques: Stitching and weaving
Divisions: Ten

Colours: Two
Design size: Two pairs of tights
3in (75mm)

1 Divide the ball into 10 with metallic thread and mark the centre line.

2 Make a marker tape to measure eighths and place pins at the $1/8$ and $2/8$ points on all the guiding threads.

3 With the first colour, complete 6 rounds using stitching method 3. To start, bring the needle up on the left of thread 1, at the $1/8$ point. Take it over to the right side of thread 2, at the $2/8$ point, then take a small stitch under thread 2 to come up on the left side, and take it up to the right side of thread 3, at the $1/8$ point and continue around the ball in the same way.

4 Work 1 more round in metallic thread.

5 Change to the second colour and repeat steps 3 and 4, but start on thread 2, at the $1/8$ point, taking the needle down to the right of thread 3, at the $2/8$ point. Lay the new threads over the previously laid threads as you stitch from the $1/8$ to the $2/8$ points, and weave them under as you stitch back up to the $1/8$ point.

6 Turn the ball so that the bottom is facing, and repeat steps 2 to 4, in the same colour scheme.

7 Using the marker tape to measure from the bottom, insert pins at the $3/8$ points on all the guiding threads.

8 Returning to the first colour, still using stitching method 3, bring the needle up on the left of thread 2, at the centre line. Take it down to the right of thread 3, at the $3/8$ point, take a stitch under thread 3 to come up on the left, and continue in this way, moving on to thread 4 at the centre line, thread 5 at the $3/8$ point, and so on. Complete the routine another 53 times,

laying all the new threads over the previously laid threads, and placing each stitch below the previous stitches. This central pattern should now meet up with the patterns at the top and bottom of the ball. (*See* below.)

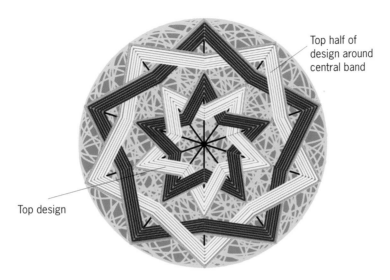

Top half of design around central band

Top design

Positioning and weaving of the inner and outer patterns.

9 Change to metallic thread to work another round.

10 Change to the second colour and repeat steps 7 and 8, this time starting on the left of thread 1, at the centre line. Weave the new threads over the previously laid threads as you stitch down from the centre line, and under as you stitch back up.

11 Turn the ball so that the top is facing and, using the marker tape from the top, insert pins at the ³⁄₈ points on all the guiding threads.

12 Repeat steps 7 to 10.

13 Change to metallic thread and make 3 long stitches to form a star in each of the negative spaces around the central band. (*See* below.)

Stitches in the negative spaces —

Central band design

Decoration in the negative spaces of the central band.

14 Weave gold thread 3 times around the guiding threads at the top and bottom, changing direction with each round to keep the weave correct.

DESIGN FIFTEEN

Difficulty rating: ✳ ✳ ✳
Techniques: Stitching and weaving
Divisions: Six

Colours: Four
Design size: Two pairs of tights
3in (75mm)

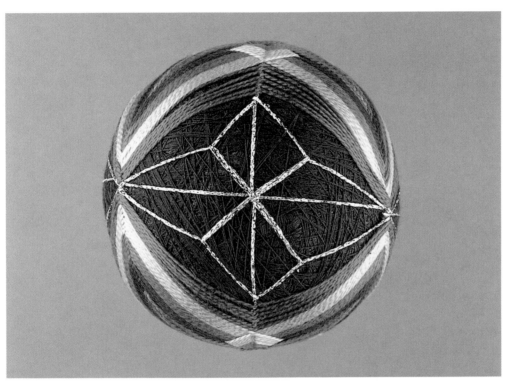

1 Divide the ball into 6 with metallic thread and mark the centre line.

2 Make a marker tape to measure quarters and place pins at the ¹/₄ and ³/₄ points on each of the guiding threads.

3 With the first colour, bring the needle up on the left of thread 1, at the ¹/₄ point. Take the needle down on the right of thread 1, as near to the top as possible, take a stitch under thread 1 to come up on the left, and then take it down on the right of thread 3, at the ¹/₄ point. Continue in this way around the ball, stitching on thread 3 at the top, on thread 5 at the ¹/₄ point and then at the top, and back to thread 1, at the ¹/₄ point. (*See* below left.) Work another 5 rounds to complete the central pattern.

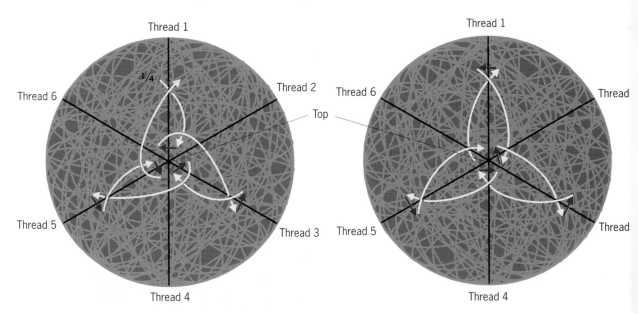

Placement and direction of stitches of central design.

Placement and direction of stitches of surrounding design.

4 Change to the second colour and work 6 rounds using stitching method 3. To start, bring the needle up on the left of thread 2, at the top, and take it down on the right of thread 3, as close as you can to the threads that have already been laid. Take a stitch under thread 3 to come up on the left, and then take the needle down on the right of thread 4, at the top. Continue in this way around the ball, stitching at thread 5 close to the previously laid threads, thread 6 at the top, thread 1 close to the previously laid threads, and finally on the right of thread 2, at the top. This completes 1 round. (*See* below left – surrounding design.) Lay all the new threads over those that have previously been laid, and place all new stitches below the previous stitches.

5 Repeat step 4 with the third colour, and then again with the fourth colour.

6 Turn the ball so that the bottom is facing, and repeat the whole process, from step 3 to step 5.

7 With the fifth colour, bring the needle up on the left of thread 1, as near as possible to the previously laid threads, and take it down on the right of thread 2, again, as near as possible to the threads that have already been laid. Take a small stitch under thread 2 to come up on the left, and then take the needle down on the right of thread 3, near the laid design. Continue in this way around the ball, taking a stitch on every thread, as close as you can to the previously laid threads. Complete 6 rounds in total, leaving a little space between each round so that the foundation threads show through.

8 Turn the ball so that the top is facing and repeat step 7.

9 Change to metallic thread and complete 1 round following the same procedure as for step 8, then turn the ball so that the bottom is facing

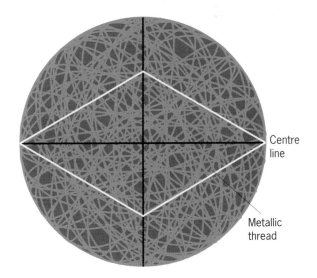

Centre line

Metallic thread

A diamond is stitched in each of the negative spaces around the ball.

once more, and work 1 more round. You will now have the outline of a diamond in metallic thread, in each negative space around the ball. (*See* illustration on previous page.)

10 Staying with the metallic thread, bring the needle up in the centre of one of these diamonds, on the left of one of the guiding threads where it crosses the centre line. Loop the thread over one of the arms of the diamond, pull slightly to draw the 'arm' in, and come back across the centre of the diamond to loop it over the opposite arm. Again, pull slightly to draw the arm in, then bring the needle back into the centre of the diamond, and take a small stitch under the threads to secure them. Repeat the routine on the other two arms of the diamond so that the diamond is pulled into a star shape, and a cross has been formed in its centre. (*See* below.)

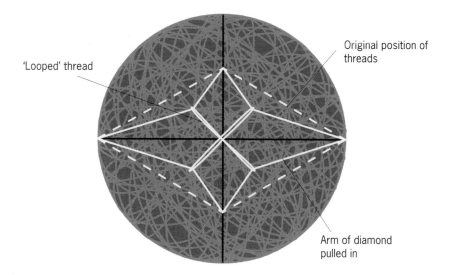

A cross stitch over the centre of the diamond pulls the arms in to form a star.

CHAPTER 8

Variations and alternative methods

DESIGN SIXTEEN

Difficulty rating: ✳ ✳
Techniques: Stitching and weaving
Divisions: Six

Colours: Three
Design size: Two pairs of tights
3in (75mm)

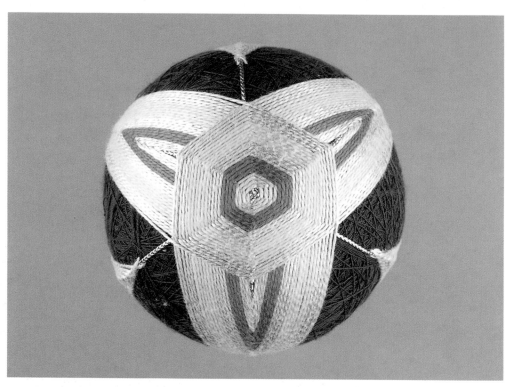

1 Divide the ball into 6 with metallic thread.

2 Make a marker tape to measure quarters, and place pins at the ¹/4 and ²/4 points on threads 1, 3 and 5.

3 With the first colour, following the illustration below left, bring the needle up at the ¹/4 point on the left of thread 1 (indicated by A), then take it down on the right side of thread 3, at the top (B). Take a stitch under thread 3 to come up on the left side (C), then take the needle over to the right side of thread 5 at the ¹/4 point (D). Pass the needle under thread 5 to come up on the left side (E), and return to thread 1, on the right side at the top (F). The illustration below right gives a representation of the pattern of stitches that should thus be formed.

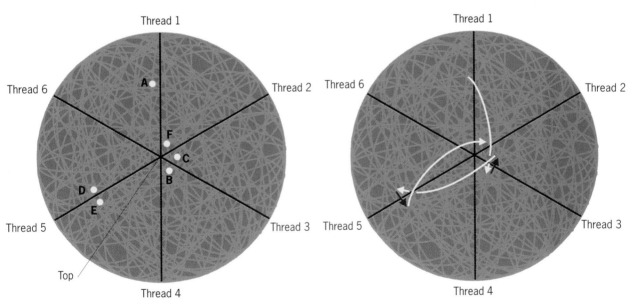

Placement and direction of stitches for the first half of 1 complete round.

The pattern of stitches formed by the first half of 1 complete round.

4 Following the diagram on page 110, complete the first round by passing the needle under thread 1 to come up on the left, at the top (G), then take it down on the right of thread 3 at the ¹/4 point (H) and pass under to come up on the left side (I). Take the needle across to thread 5 and down on the right

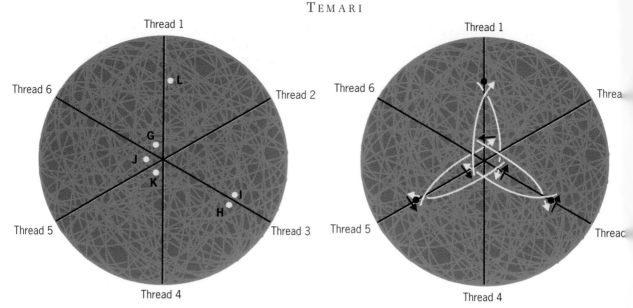

Placement and direction of stitches for the second half of 1 complete round.

The pattern formed at the completion of 1 round.

side at the top (J), then pass it under and up on the left side (K) and finally, down on the right side of thread 1, at the ¼ point (L). (*See* the illustration above right for a representation of the complete round.)

5 Work 3 more complete rounds in the first colour.

6 Change to the second colour and work 4 more complete rounds.

7 Back with the first colour, work 4 rounds.

8 Work 6 rounds in the third colour.

9 In the first colour again, work 5 more rounds. At this stage, the design should have reached the ¾ point on threads 1, 3, and 5.

10 Turn the ball so that the bottom is facing you and repeat the whole design, working on threads 2, 4 and 6.

DESIGN SEVENTEEN

Difficulty rating: ✳ ✳   Colours: Four
Techniques: Stitching and weaving   Design size: Two pairs of tights
Divisions: Ten   3in (75mm)

1 Divide the ball into 10 with metallic thread.

2 Make a marker tape to measure quarters and place pins at the ¼ points on all the guiding threads.

3 With the first colour, bring the needle up as near to the top as possible, on the left of thread 1. Using a variation of stitching method 1, take the thread over to the right of thread 3, then back under to come up on the left side, then over to thread 5. Continue in the same way on threads 7 and 9, and return to thread 1. This completes 1 round. Work 6 more rounds.

4 When you reach thread 10 on round 7, take the needle over threads 1, 2, and 3 and down on the right of thread 4, at the ¼ point. This thread has to lie against those already laid, so use them as a guide. Take the needle under and up to the left of thread 4, then over threads 5, 6 and 7 and down on the

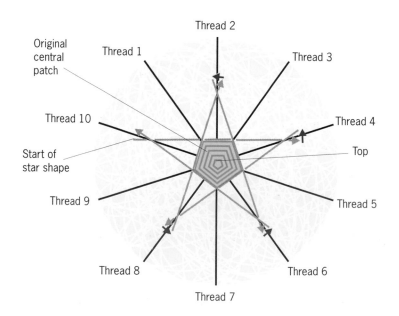

Placement and direction of stitches.

right of thread 8, under and up to the left, over 9, 10 and 1, and down on the right of thread 2, under, up and over 3, 4, and 5 to go down on the right of thread 6, and finally under, up and over threads 7, 8 and 9 to go down on the right of thread 10. This completes the first round of the star shape (*see* the illustration below left for a representation of the shape formed). Complete 3 more rounds in the first colour.

5 Change to the second colour and repeat step 4.

6 Change to the third colour and repeat step 4.

7 Change to the fourth colour and repeat step 4.

8 Turn the ball so that the bottom is facing and repeat steps 2 to 7, starting this time on the left of thread 2, so that the points of the star come up between the points of the original star.

9 With the fourth colour, bring the needle up on the left of any one of the guiding threads, as close as possible to one of the points of either design. From this point work 3 rounds using stitching method 3. To begin, take the needle down on the right of the next thread, pass the needle under the guiding thread to come up on the left, then take it up again to the point of the first design on the right of the next guiding thread. Lay all the new threads over the previously laid threads, and place the new threads below the other threads at the top and the bottom so that a plait forms at the top and a 'v' forms at the bottom.

10 Repeat step 9 another 4 times; once with the first colour, once with the second, then the third, and finally with the fourth.

DESIGN EIGHTEEN

Difficulty rating: ✳ ✳
Techniques: Stitching and weaving
Divisions: Sixteen

Colours: Four
Design size: Two pairs of tights
3in (75mm)

1 Divide the ball into 16 with metallic thread and mark the centre line.

2 Make a marker tape to measure sixths and attach it to the top of the ball so that it can rotate. Place pins at the ²/₆ and ⁴/₆ points on thread 2.

3 With the first colour, bring the needle up at the centre line, on the left of thread 1. Working to the right, take the needle over to the ²/₆ point on the right of thread 2 (indicated by A on the illustration right). Take a small stitch under the thread to come up on the left side, then down to the centre line on the right of thread 3. Turn the ball 90° clockwise and take the thread to the ⁴/₆ point on the right of thread 2 (B), then under and up on the left. Turn the ball a further 90° clockwise and take the thread back to the centre line on the right of thread 1, and then back to A to complete the first diamond shape. Complete 3 more rounds.

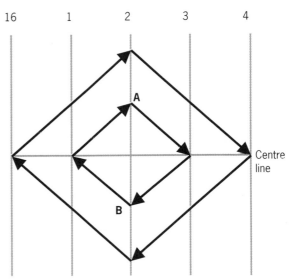

Placement and direction of stitches for basic diamond shape. The diamond will stretch from thread 16 to thread 4 when all the threads have been laid.

4 Repeat step 3 with the second colour.

5 Change to the third colour and repeat step 3 again.

6 Repeat step 3 once more, this time with the fourth colour.

7 Swivel the marker tape to place the pins at the ²/₆ and ⁴/₆ points on thread 4 and repeat steps 3 to 6, starting on the left of thread 3 at the centre line. As you take the needle over from thread 3 to thread 4, lay the new threads over the previously laid threads, and as you take the needle back from thread 4 to thread 3, weave the new threads under. (*See* the illustration below for the weaving pattern.)

The system of weaving.

8 Repeat step 7, swivelling the marker tape to thread 6, and starting on the left of thread 5. Repeat 4 more times, marking threads 8, 10, 12 and 14 and starting on threads 7, 9, 11 and 13.

9 Mark thread 16 in the same way and follow the same process starting from thread 15, but as this diamond overlaps the first diamond, there is more weaving required. As you take the needle from thread 15 to thread 16, lay the new threads over those previously laid, weave them under as you stitch from thread 16 to thread 1, over as you return from thread 1 to thread 16, and under from thread 16 to thread 15.

10 Outline the whole pattern with the metallic thread, following the same weaving system, to complete the design. A star pattern is created at the top and bottom of the ball, and the guiding threads should all radiate from the points in the design.

DESIGN NINETEEN

Difficulty rating: ✳ ✳ ✳
Techniques: Stitching and weaving
Divisions: Twelve

Colours: Four
Design size: Two pairs of tights
3in (75mm)

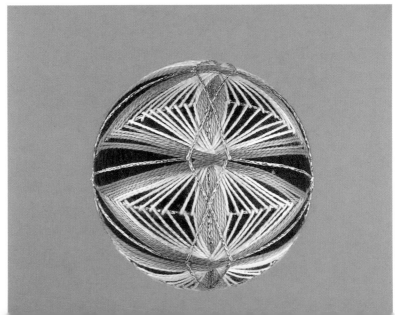

1 Divide the ball into 12 with metallic thread and mark the centre line.

2 Wind 1 round of metallic thread around each side of the centre line, taking a small stitch under the threads from one side to the other, and then wind the first colour 5 times around each side.

3 Change to the second colour and bring the needle up on the left of thread 1, at the edge of the central band. Take the needle over the band, crossing thread 2 on the centre line, then take it down on the right of thread 3, at the edge of the central band. Take a small stitch under this thread to come up on the left, then take the needle back over the central band and down at its edge on the right of thread 5. Continue in this way around the ball, stitching on threads 7, 9, 11 and back to 1. Work another 7 rounds in the same way, leaving a small space between each stitch on consecutive rounds, so that the foundation threads show through. (*See* below.)

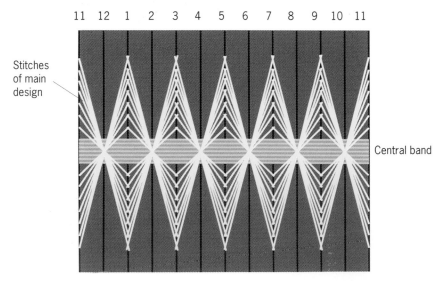

The main pattern crosses on the centre line on the even-numbered threads.

4 Turn the ball so that the bottom is facing and repeat step 3, still using the second colour.

5 Change to the third colour and repeat steps 3 and 4, but work only 3 rounds for each.

6 Change to the fourth colour and repeat steps 3 and 4, but work only 2 rounds for each.

7 Change to metallic thread and bring the needle up on the left of thread 2, as close to the previously laid threads as possible: your stitch will be slightly out from the central band. Take it over the central band, crossing the centre line on thread 3, and down on the right of thread 4. Take a stitch under the thread to come up on the left side, then take the needle back over the central band, and down on the right of thread 6. Continue around the ball in the same way, stitching on threads 8, 10, 12 and back to 2, then turn the ball so that the bottom is facing, and repeat the process from the other side. (*See* below.)

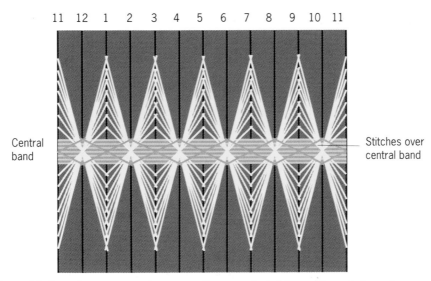

The gold threads cross on the centre line on the odd-numbered threads.

8 Weave metallic thread about 5 times around the guiding threads at the top and bottom to make a small rosette, changing direction with each round to keep the weave correct.

DESIGN TWENTY

Difficulty rating: ✳ ✳ ✳

Techniques: Stitching

Divisions: Sixteen

Colours: Six

Design size: Two pairs of tights
3in (75mm)

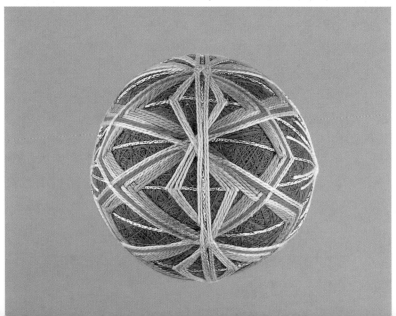

1 Divide the ball into 16 with metallic thread and mark the centre line.

2 Make a marking tape to measure quarters and place pins at the ¹/4, ²/4 and ³/4 points on each guiding thread.

3 With the first colour, using a variation of stitching method 3, bring the needle up on the left of thread 1, at the ¹/4 point. Take the needle over the ²/4 point on thread 3 and down on the right of thread 5, at the ³/4 point. Take a small stitch under thread 5 from right to left, then take the needle over the ²/4 point on thread 7 and up to the right of thread 9, at the ¹/4 point. Following the same routine, take the needle down to thread 13 and back up to thread 1. Stitch 2 complete rounds in this way. Place the stitches at the ¹/4 points above the previous stitches and the stitches at the ³/4 points below, and cross the threads over from one side of the previously laid threads to the other at the centre line (*see* below). This will form a 'v' at the top and bottom points of the design.

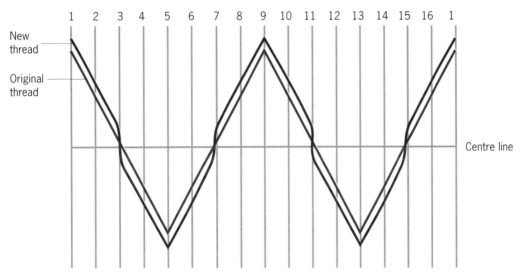

New threads must be crossed from one side of the previous thread to the other as they are laid.

4 Repeat step 3 another 3 times, starting at the ¹/4 point on the left of thread 3 for the first repeat, on the left of thread 5 for the second, and on the left of thread 7 for the third.

5 Change to the second colour and repeat steps 3 and 4.

6 Repeat step 5 another 3 times, changing to the third colour for the first repeat, to the fourth colour for the second repeat, and to the fifth for the third and final repeat.

7 Return to the first colour and bring the needle up midway between the ¹/₄ and the ²/₄ points on the left of thread 2. Take the thread over the centre line to the right of thread 4, midway between the ²/₄ and ³/₄ points, take the needle under thread 4 and up on the left, then over the centre line to the right of thread 6, midway between the ¹/₄ and ²/₄ points. Continue in this way around the ball, laying all the new threads over the previously laid threads. Work 2 complete rounds.

8 Turn the ball so that the bottom is facing and repeat step 7.

9 Change to the fifth colour and repeat steps 7 and 8.

10 Return to the third colour, wind it twice around one side of the centre line, take a stitch under the threads to come up on the other side of the centre line, and then wind it twice around that side.

11 Change to the sixth colour and make long stitches in the negative spaces between each of the guiding threads at the top and the bottom. (*See* right.)

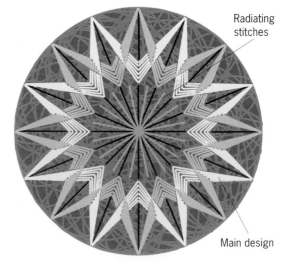

Radiating stitches

Main design

The negative spaces at the top and bottom of the ball are filled with radiating stitches.

DESIGN TWENTY-ONE

Difficulty rating: ✳ ✳ ✳
Techniques: Stitching and winding
Divisions: Ten

Colours: Six
Design size: Two pairs of tights
3in (75mm)

1 Divide the ball into 10 with metallic thread and mark the centre line.

2 Make a marker tape to measure quarters and place pins at all these points on the guiding threads.

3 Weave 3 rounds of metallic thread over and under the guiding threads at the top and bottom, stitching clockwise on the first round, anticlockwise on the second, and clockwise again on the third, to keep the weave correct.

4 With the first colour, stitch 6 complete rounds using a variation of stitching method 1. To start, bring the needle up on the left of thread 1, next to the woven central circle. Take the needle over to the right of thread 3, keeping the threads close to the central circle. Continue in this way, taking the needle over to thread 5, 7, 9, and then back to 1. This will form a pentagon. (*See* below.)

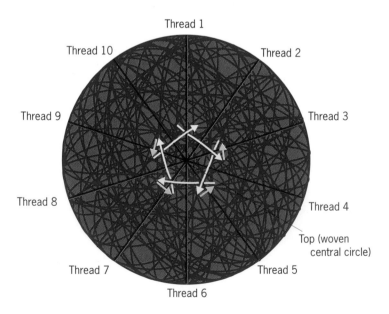

The pentagon formed using stitching method 1.

5 Add 1 round of metallic thread.

6 Where A refers to all the points next to the central circle and B to all the ¼ points on the guiding threads, take the second colour and bring the needle up on the left of thread 1, at point B. Take it over to the right of thread 4, at point A, then take it under thread 4, up on the left and over to the right of thread 7, at point B, then under, up and over to the right of thread 10, at point A. From there take it under, up and over to thread 3 at point B, and continue in this way around the ball, finishing at thread 1, point B. This will form a star shape (see below). Follow this routine 3 more times, making firm anchor stitches around the guiding threads, and keeping the middle neat. There will be 8 threads around the central circle.

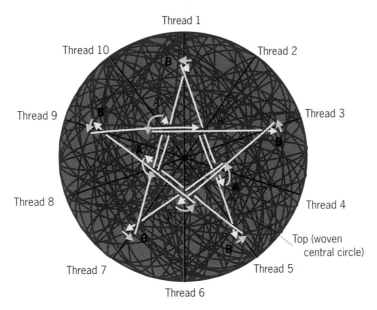

Placement and direction of stitches to form the star shape.

7 With metallic thread, and using stitching method 1, work 1 round, starting on thread 2 and stitching over threads 4, 6, 8, 10 and back to 2, to form another pentagon.

8 With the third colour, complete 4 rounds following the same routine as for step 6, but begin at thread 2, point A, then go to 5B, 8A, 1B, 4A, 7B, 10A, 3B, 6A, 9B and back to 2A.

9 Return to the metallic thread and to stitching method 1 to work another pentagon, stitching on threads 1, 3, 5, 7, 9 and back to 1.

10 Repeat steps 6 to 9, using the fourth colour for step 6 and the fifth colour for step 8.

11 Repeat steps 6 to 9 again, returning to the first colour for step 6, then changing to the sixth colour for step 8.

12 Turn the ball so that the bottom is facing and repeat the whole design, from step 3 to step 11.

13 Turn the ball to work around the centre line. Wind the fifth colour 4 times around one side of the centre line, then take a stitch under the threads and wind it 4 times around the other side.

14 Change to the second colour and wind 3 times around each side of the central band.

15 Anchor these wound threads with stitches, in the third colour, crossing over the band, taking a stitch at each of the guiding threads. Start on one side of the band and work around the ball, then turn the ball to do the same starting on the other side. This will form a series of diamonds as shown on the illustration right.

16 Work 3 more rounds of diamonds, in the fourth colour, crossing over the central band. In the negative spaces, find the midline between the guiding threads (this runs through the crossing points of the first set of diamonds), and the $^1/_6$, $^2/_6$ and $^3/_6$ points between the central band and the inverted points of the star shape along this line. Stitch the first round of diamonds from the $^1/_6$ point on one side of the band to the $^1/_6$ point on the other, stitch the second round from the $^2/_6$ to the $^2/_6$, and stitch the third round from the $^3/_6$ to the $^3/_6$ point. (*See* below.)

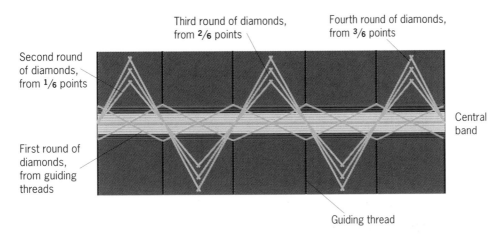

Decoration on central band.

DESIGN TWENTY-TWO

Difficulty rating: ✳ ✳ ✳
Techniques: Stitching and weaving
Divisions: Twelve

Colours: Two
Design size: Two pairs of tights
        3in (75mm)

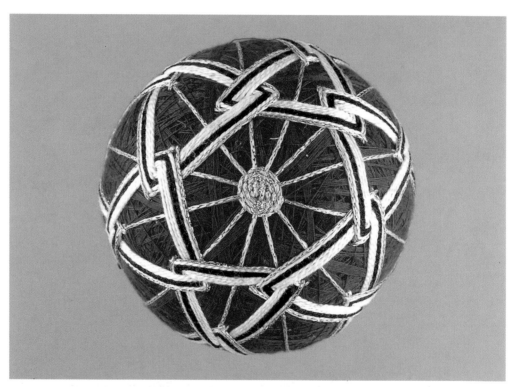

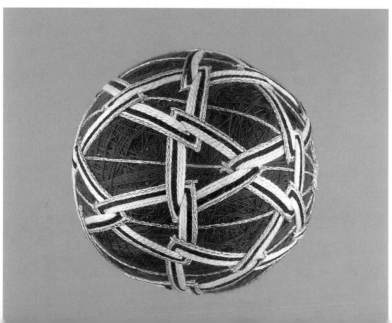

1 Divide the ball into 12 with metallic thread.

2 Make a marker tape to measure sixths. Place pins at the ¹⁄₆ points on threads 1, 3, 5, 7, 9 and 11, and at the ²⁄₆ points on threads 2, 4, 6, 8, 10 and 12. Remove the pins as you work.

3 With the first colour, bring the needle up on the left of thread 1, at the ¹⁄₆ point. Take the needle down on the right of thread 3, at the ¹⁄₆ point, then under thread 3 to come up on the left. From here, take the needle over to the right of thread 2, at the ²⁄₆ point, under and up on the left, then over to the right of thread 1, at the ¹⁄₆ point. Complete this routine 3 times with the first colour, twice with the second, and then once more with the first. (*See above right.*)

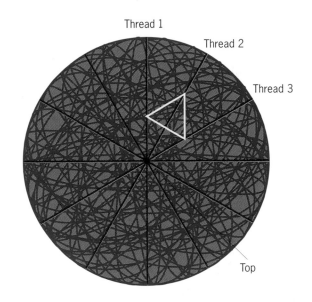

Stitching the first triangle.

4 Repeat step 3, working on threads 3, 4 and 5. Bring the needle up at the ¹⁄₆ point on the left of thread 3, take it over the previously laid threads and down at the ¹⁄₆ point on thread 5, down to the ²⁄₆ point on thread 4, and back under the previously laid threads to the ¹⁄₆ point on thread 3.

5 When the triangle in step 4 has been completed, continue around the top of the ball in the same manner (starting on threads 5, 7, 9 and 11) to form 6 interlocking triangles. These will form a hexagon around the top of the ball.

6 Turn the ball to work on the other half. Place pins at the ¹⁄₆ points on threads 2, 4, 6, 8, 10 and 12, then place a second round of pins at the ²⁄₆ points on threads 1, 3, 5, 7, 9 and 11.

7 Repeat steps 2 to 5.

8 Using the marker tape, place pins at the ³⁄₆ points in the centre of each of the divisions.

9 With the first colour, bring the needle up at the ²⁄₆ point on any of the threads and work a triangle with the points here and at the ³⁄₆ points indicated by the pins. Work around the ball as in step 3, taking the new threads over and then under the previously laid threads. (*See* below.)

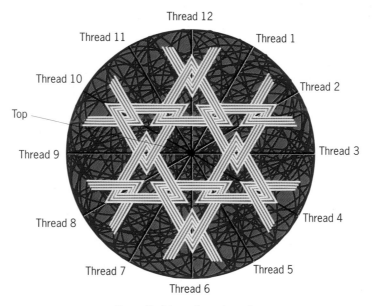

Thread 12
Thread 11
Thread 1
Thread 10
Thread 2
Top
Thread 9
Thread 3
Thread 8
Thread 4
Thread 7
Thread 5
Thread 6

Interlinking the triangles.

10 Turn the ball so that the top is facing once more, and repeat steps 8 and 9.

11 Weave metallic thread around the top and bottom about 5 times, working alternately clockwise and then anticlockwise for each round to keep the weaving pattern correct.

12 Outline all the triangles with metallic thread, following the weaving pattern that has been set.

Free embroidery

A TEMARI ball offers a suitable surface for any embroidery and many free designs work well: leaves, flowers and birds in particular lend themselves to the circular shape. You can even incorporate other materials such as beads, as shown in the samples. The choice is yours.

Right *These leaves have been embroidered using crewel wool, with beads added for extra texture.*

Far right *Bullion knots form the rose petals in this design, with stem stitch and lazy daisy stitch used for the leaves and stems.*

Below left *Lazy daisy stitch is used again for the leaves and petals, with French knots forming the flower centres.*

Below right *Couched chenille thread gives a tactile dragonfly!*

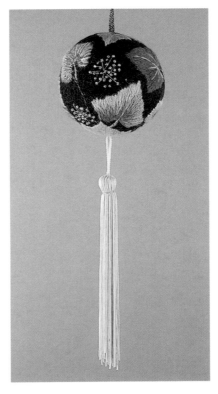

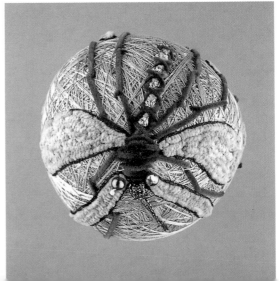

About the author

MARGARET LUDLOW has had a long-term interest in art, silk painting and embroidery. When the last of her children left home in 1980 she began a City and Guilds course in Embroidery and Design and followed this with an adult teachers' training course in 1984. She has since been teaching embroidery techniques in England and Malaysia, where she was introduced to the craft of temari.

Margaret's own work is centred on ceremonial pieces such as military colours, Masonic and promotional banners, ecclesiastic vestments and furnishings. She is a life member of the Embroiderers' Guild.

Margaret with her first temari creation!

WITHDRAWN

TOYMAKING

Designing & Making Wooden Toys	*Terry Kelly*	Making Wooden Toys & Games	*Jeff & Jennie Loader*
Fun to Make Wooden Toys & Games	*Jeff & Jennie Loader*	Restoring Rocking Horses	*Clive Green & Anthony Dew*
Making Board, Peg & Dice Games	*Jeff & Jennie Loader*		

DOLLS' HOUSES

Architecture for Dolls' Houses	*Joyce Percival*	Making Miniature Oriental Rugs & Carpets	*Meik & Ian McNaughton*
Beginners' Guide to the Dolls' House Hobby	*Jean Nisbett*	Making Period Dolls' House Accessories	*Andrea Barham*
The Complete Dolls' House Book	*Jean Nisbett*	Making Period Dolls' House Furniture	*Derek & Sheila Rowbottom*
Dolls' House Bathrooms: Lots of Little Loos	*Patricia King*	Making Tudor Dolls' Houses	*Derek Rowbottom*
Easy to Make Dolls' House Accessories	*Andrea Barham*	Making Unusual Miniatures	*Graham Spalding*
Make Your Own Dolls' House Furniture	*Maurice Harper*	Making Victorian Dolls' House Furniture	*Patricia King*
Making Dolls' House Furniture	*Patricia King*	Miniature Needlepoint Carpets	*Janet Granger*
Making Georgian Dolls' Houses	*Derek Rowbottom*	The Secrets of the Dolls' House Makers	*Jean Nisbett*

CRAFTS

Celtic Knotwork Designs	*Sheila Sturrock*	Making Greetings Cards for Beginners	*Pat Sutherland*
Collage from Seeds, Leaves and Flowers	*Joan Carver*	Making Knitwear Fit	*Pat Ashforth & Steve Plummer*
Complete Pyrography	*Stephen Poole*	Needlepoint: A Foundation Course	*Sandra Hardy*
Creating Knitwear Designs	*Pat Ashforth & Steve Plummer*	Pyrography Handbook (Practical Crafts)	*Stephen Poole*
Cross Stitch Kitchen Projects	*Janet Granger*	Tassel Making for Beginners	*Enid Taylor*
Cross Stitch on Colour	*Sheena Rogers*	Tatting Collage	*Lindsay Rogers*
Embroidery Tips & Hints	*Harold Hayes*	Temari: A Traditional Japanese	
An Introduction to Crewel Embroidery	*Mave Glenny*	Embroidery Technique	*Margaret Ludlow*
Making Character Bears	*Valerie Tyler*		

THE HOME

Home Ownership: Buying and Maintaining	*Nicholas Snelling*	Security for the Householder:	
		Fitting Locks and Other Devices	*E. Phillips*

VIDEOS

Drop-in and Pinstuffed Seats	*David James*	Twists and Advanced Turning	*Dennis White*
Stuffover Upholstery	*David James*	Sharpening the Professional Way	*Jim Kingshott*
Elliptical Turning	*David Springett*	Sharpening Turning & Carving Tools	*Jim Kingshott*
Woodturning Wizardry	*David Springett*	Bowl Turning	*John Jordan*
Turning Between Centres: The Basics	*Dennis White*	Hollow Turning	*John Jordan*
Turning Bowls	*Dennis White*	Woodturning: A Foundation Course	*Keith Rowley*
Boxes, Goblets and Screw Threads	*Dennis White*	Carving a Figure: The Female Form	*Ray Gonzalez*
Novelties and Projects	*Dennis White*	The Router: A Beginner's Guide	*Alan Goodsell*
Classic Profiles	*Dennis White*	The Scroll Saw: A Beginner's Guide	*John Burke*

MAGAZINES

WOODTURNING ◆ WOODCARVING ◆ TOYMAKING
FURNITURE & CABINETMAKING ◆ BUSINESSMATTERS
CREATIVE IDEAS FOR THE HOME ◆ THE ROUTER

———————————◆———————————

The above represents a full list of all titles currently published or scheduled to be published. All are available direct from the Publishers or through bookshops, newsagents and specialist retailers. To place an order, or to obtain a complete catalogue, contact:

GMC Publications,
166 High Street, Lewes, East Sussex BN7 1XU, United Kingdom
Tel: 01273 488005 Fax: 01273 478606

Orders by credit card are accepted